INTEGRATION OF
PHYSICAL EDUCATION IN THE
ELEMENTARY SCHOOL CURRICULUM

ABOUT THE AUTHOR

James H. Humphrey, Professor Emeritus at the University of Maryland, has published over 40 book and 200 articles and research reports. He has also written 13 children's books and produced four educational record albums.

An advocate for the integration of physical education in the elementary school curriculum, his statements on the subject have been translated into four languages and distributed to 55 countries. In addition, his work in this area has been featured on a Voice of America broadcast and distributed to their 35 language centers.

INTEGRATION OF PHYSICAL EDUCATION IN THE ELEMENTARY SCHOOL CURRICULUM

By

JAMES H. HUMPHREY, ED.D.

Professor Emeritus
University of Maryland

With a Foreword by

David H. Clarke, Ph.D.

Professor and Chairman
Department of Kinesiology
University of Maryland

CHARLES C THOMAS • PUBLISHER
Springfield • Illinois • U.S.A.

Published and Distributed Throughout the World by

CHARLES C THOMAS • PUBLISHER
2600 South First Street
Springfield, Illinois 62794-9265

© *1990 by* CHARLES C THOMAS • PUBLISHER
ISBN 0-398-05707-9
Library of Congress Catalog Card Number: 90-39749

Printed in the United States of America
SC-R-3

Library of Congress Cataloging-in-Publication Data

Humphrey, James Harry, 1911–
    Integration of physical education in the elementary school
curriculum / by James H. Humphrey ; with a foreword by David H.
Clarke.
      p. cm.
    Includes bibliographical references and index.
    ISBN 0-398-05707-9
    1. Physical education for children—United States—Curricula.
2. Education, Elementary—United States—Curricula. I. Title.
GV443.H815   1990
372.86'043—dc20
                                      90-39749
                                       CIP

FOREWORD

The reader who has been conditioned to think of the elementary school curriculum as just a series of specific subjects will view this text with enthusiasm for the possibilities of enhancing comtemporary education. The theory is sound and the alternatives for meaningful elementary school education are endless. James Humphrey has provided a forum for the justification of physical education that should receive the most serious consideration by both professional educators and the public at large. While it is usual to think that a variety of games and activities are important to the young child, it is nevertheless unusual to think that they can actually be integrated into the total school curriculum in a planned and meaningful way. This book provides a blueprint for just such a proposal.

James H. Humphrey has devoted a lifetime to the pursuit of excellence in health and physical education programs for school-aged children. He has written more extensively than any other professional educator on these and related subjects, and this text is the capstone of a brilliant career. We can all learn from the lessons embodied in this plan, but more specifically the direction suggested should be carefully considered by those professionals directly involved in curriculum planning. How exciting to contemplate the serious integration of various traditional subject matter fields with physical education.

Professor Humphrey entered physical education, as many before him and since, as an athlete. The first-hand exposure to the many possibilities inherent in this field took place naturally, and was eventually followed by a desire to be able to participate in the educational process of prospective teachers and coaches. Little did he know then that he would engage in a lifetime of inquiry and teaching that would span several decades and involve countless hundreds of students preparing themselves for teaching careers. His ability to expose these individuals to the most modern concepts of sport and physical education has served to upgrade not only physical education but all of education.

The concepts proposed are articulated from years of experience in research and curriculum development. The author has not only written extensively about the subject matter but has been responsible for developing the line of research investigation that has made this treatise possible. In other words, the ideas presented have been tested in public forum in the academic community. Now they have been compiled and made available in a form that permits implementation in the nation's schools. The reader will find them fascinating and thought-provoking. If the interest lies in assisting young people to a more meaningful education, James Humphrey's latest text should be required reading.

David H. Clarke, Ph.D.

INTRODUCTION

O ver the years I have often been asked how I first became interested in the integration of physical education in the elementary school curriculum. In fact, this interest probably began before I actually realized it.

In the mid 1940s I became a supervisor of physical education in a midwestern city school system at a time in the immediate post World War II era when many school systems were expanding their physical education program, particularly at the elementary school level. It was a major part of my job to inaugurate a program of physical education in the elementary schools where there were little or no facilities for this purpose, or special teachers of physical education. This, of course, meant that the entire teaching responsibility fell to the already overburdened classroom teachers, and under conditions that required extraordinary imagination and creativeness. It was then that with the assistance of some classroom teachers, that I developed the idea of relating physical education experiences to the other subject areas.

The plan took hold immediately because classroom teachers were able to see the value of physical education as a medium to help children learn skills and concepts in other curriculum areas.

For over a period of four decades I have been able to engage in a great deal of research and widespread field testing and experimentation in this general area. These experiences have been incorporated into over 30 publications on the subject in the form of books, articles, research reports, and position papers. And, now with additional experimentation, research, and updating, I have drawn all these materials together to comprise the present volume.

The first chapter presents a general overview of the elementary school curriculum, taking into account such factors as the modern meaning and concept of curriculum and approaches to curriculum development. In addition, there are discussions of the curriculum areas most frequently provided on a daily basis in the average elementary school—reading, writing, mathematics, science, and social studies.

Chapter 2 deals with physical education in the elementary school with regard to such factors as historical development and trends, concepts of child development and their meaning for physical education, objectives of physical education, the planning of physical education experiences for children, the teaching-learning situation in elementary school physical education and planning physical education lessons.

In Chapter 3 there is a detailed account of the nature of integration in physical education. Included here are discussions of the three aspects of educational integration—psychological, sociological, and pedagogical. Other important topics discussed in this chapter are the advantages of integrating physical education in the elementary school curriculum, teaching responsibility, and cognitive physical education as the approach best suited for integrating physical education.

Integration of physical education and reading is the subject of Chapter 4 and considers reading diagnosis through physical education experiences, teaching reading skills and concepts through physical education and the AMAV concept, a technique developed by the author for the purpose of teaching children to read and to improve their reading ability through the physical education medium.

Other facets of language arts comprises Chapter 5 and includes ways in which physical education experiences can be integrated with listening, speaking, and writing.

In Chapter 6 the mathematical processes considered for integration with physical education are number and numeration systems, the arithmetical operations of addition, subtraction, multiplication, and division, and the various dimensions of geometry. There is also a discussion of the use of mathematics physical education, listening, and reading content.

Several areas of science and physical education integration are presented in Chapter 7. These include the universe and earth, conditions of life, and chemical and physical changes. Several examples of science physical education stories are also included.

In the final chapter the integration of physical education and social studies gives consideration to the place of physical education in social studies units, as well as several physical education activities with inherent social studies concepts.

A book is seldom the sole product of the author. Granted, the author does most of the things concerned with actually putting a book together. However, it is almost always true that many individuals participate, at least indirectly, in some way before a book is finally "put to bed." This volume is no exception.

To acknowledge everyone personally would be practically impossible—for example, the countless numbers of teachers and children with whom I have been associated with over the years to whom I would like to express a debt of gratitude collectively.

It is possible and practical, however, to cite certain individuals personally. The following persons shared knowledge with me on what certain parts of the book were based which would otherwise have been impossible: Virginia Moore, former Supervisor of Elementary Education, Anne Arundel County, Maryland Public Schools, Robert Ashlock, former Director of the Arithmetic Center at the University of Maryland, Robert Wilson, Director of the Reading Center at the University of Maryland, and Dorothy Sullivan, former Associate Professor of Education at the University of Maryland. At one time or another all of these individuals have been coauthors with me on a variety of writing projects.

CONTENTS

INTEGRATION OF
PHYSICAL EDUCATION IN THE
ELEMENTARY SCHOOL CURRICULUM

Chapter 1

THE ELEMENTARY SCHOOL CURRICULUM

The term *curriculum* has been used in a number of different ways over the years and the result has been a misunderstanding as to what the scope of the curriculum actually entails. In the past, in some cases the curriculum has been confused with the course of study and as a result these two terms have been used interchangably to convey an identical meaning. However, it should be understood that the curriculum is very broad in scope and that the course of study is actually an outgrowth of curriculum development.

The *Dictionary of Education* defines the elementary school curriculum as "the sum total of educative activities in which pupils engage under the auspices of the elementary school." Of course these educative activities should be guided, supervised, and directed in such a way that they are channeled toward the achievement of the objectives of the elementary school.

HISTORICAL DEVELOPMENT OF THE CURRICULUM

Although the development of the elementary school curriculum over the years has been characterized by various degree of criticism, it can be said that for the most part attempts have been made to gear the curriculum to meet the needs of the times. For example, in the early common schools the so-called three Rs seemed to be sufficient tools for the citzenry of that era.

As the common schools developed there appeared to be a decreasing interest in curriculum offerings and a greater abundance of interest in such phases of school administration as procurement of funds, suitable housing, and recruitment of teachers.

By the end of the 19th century it was becoming increasingly clear that a curriculum consisting only of the three Rs would not be sufficient to meet the continuing social needs of a changing America. With elementary education the terminal education for large numbers of individuals and with the need for citizens to take their place in a democracy in a rapidly changing culture, a reevaluation of the elementary school curriculum was inevitable. There followed an influx of new subjects seeking admittance into the elementary school curriculum family and as a result there occurred a source of controversy that was to last for some years to come.

After 1900 there developed a period in our educational history that was characterized by the injection of the idea that the elementary school curriculum should be organized on a scientific basis. With emphasis being placed upon different kinds of teaching methods based on psychological principles of learning, there were proposals that the subject-matter areas of the elementary school curriculum be improved. Unfortunately, at the time the curriculum was thought of largely only in terms of subject-matter areas. As a consequence, it was believed, no doubt erroneously, that the obviously simple answer to curriculum improvement could be found in the addition of various new subjects to the elementary school program.

During the 20th century perhaps the greatest single change in the elementary school curriculum has been concerned with curriculum organization. Typical subject organizations sometimes have tended to be replaced by various kinds of units and projects. Proponents for this type of transition believed that this procedure tended to place the emphasis on a child-centered curriculum as opposed to a subject-centered curriculum.

In the past, in far too many instances tradition has been substituted for scientific procedures in undertaking curriculum development at the elementary school level. In a changing culture which places the child in a complex web of environmental forces, it may be readily discerned that emphasis should be placed on the development of the individual and that subject-matter areas are merely a means to that end rather than the end itself.

A Modern Concept of Curriculum

It has taken some time to arrive at the present-day concept of the elementary school curriculum. A "lag" which has caused the elementary school curriculum to be interpreted only in terms of subject matter has been partly responsible for this condition. A more modern approach to an understanding of the place of subjects in the curriculum is that learning which results from the experiences in the various subjects, rather than the subjects themselves, should be considered as the real curriculum content.

The modern elementary school curriculum is also characterized by the attention that is given to the principles of growth and development of children as well as the fact that learning takes place better when learning activities operate in the real experience. (As will be seen in later chapters, physical education can make a tremendous contribution to this endeavor). In addition, the acception of integration as an educational concept which accentuates the wholeness and unity of the child is inherent in the better-than-average elementary school curriculum of today.

Another modern point of view is that there may be several curriculums making up the total curriculum. For example, in virtually all modern elementary schools the basic three Rs (reading, 'riting, and 'rithmetic) are offered as more or less separate curriculum areas. (Large numbers of schools provide for a language arts curriculum which includes the various facets of communication—reading, writing, listening, and speaking). Also a great many provide for a science curriculum and a social studies curriculum. And to a lesser extent there are curriculum areas in art, music, and physical education.

In view of the fact that the present-day elementary school curriculum embraces all of organized experiences under the guidance of the school, in reality there are no "extracuricular" activities. This does not imply that there should be no other activities except those that take place in the regular classroom. On the contrary, there will be many additional activities in the form of after-school recreational activities, various kinds of clubs, and the like. When the elementary school curriculum is viewed in the broad sense, these activities should be referred to as "extraclass" activities rather than "extracurricular" activities inasmuch as they should be considered a part of the total school curriculum.

APPROACHES TO CURRICULUM DEVELOPMENT

There have been a variety of theories and opinions set forth regarding elementary school curriculum organization. As a consequence, it might be expected that approaches to curriculum development have presented one of the foremost challenges to the area of elementary education.

Through the years, in spite of the fact that the curriculum lag has been such that it has never really caught up with societal needs, there has been some crystallization of thinking with regard to curriculum organization.

Although some educators as well as laymen have been somewhat disturbed by the curriculum lag, on the other hand, there are those persons who have resisted curriculum reorganization quite vigorously. The result has been the development of a sort of educational phenomenon which finds proponents who hold tenaciously to certain more or less prejudiced beliefs regarding approaches to curriculum development.

It should be obvious that there are certain advantages and disadvantages of any type of curriculum organization when that particular organization is employed in absolute form. It is for this reason that many modern educators prefer to select procedures from various forms of curriculum organization and then adapt as best they can to meet local needs.

It should be understood that there are certain constant features in any type of curriculum organization and that adjustments should be made accordingly on the basis of the needs of the children in a specific community. For instance, all types of curriculum organization should be designed to orient learning experiences in such a way that these experiences make an optimum contribution to the total growth and development of elementary school children. Consequently, the primary problem of curriculum development concerns ways and means of making school learning experiences beneficial and worthwhile to children. There are a number of versions of curriculum organization through which this objective might be accomplished in specific situations. However, it should be mentioned that all versions should be taken into consideration and the best ideas from each might well be taken and adapted to the local situation. The reader should view the subsequent discussions of the various versions of curriculum organization with this idea in mind. In other words, the main purpose here will be to familiarize the reader with some of the advantages and limitations of the various versions of curriculum organization, particularly when any one version is employed in absolute form to the exclusion of certain of the desirable elements of the other versions.

The Subject Version of Curriculum Organization

The term *subject* has a number of vastly different dictionary meanings. As it relates to education a subject has been considered as "one of the branches of learning." Thought of in these terms, there could perhaps be no restriction put on the number of possible subjects that could be legitimately considered as school subject-matter areas. As might well be expected, one of the great dangers in this interpretation lies in the fact that theoretically, at least, the curriculum could become overcrowded to the extent that it would be next to impossible to provide for individual differences of children.

A typical list of subjects for an elementary school might consist of reading, other language arts, mathematics, science, social studies, art, music, and physical education. An allegedly important feature about a subject is its specificity and uniqueness in relation to other subjects. In fact, in some cases some of the subjects,[1] such as art, music, and physical education, have been considered so utterly different that they have been classified as "special subjects." In the case of physical education, under most circumstances it has been thought of only as being special with regard to teaching responsibility, when in reality any "special" qualities that this area of the curriculum might have would be in the realm of facilities, materials, and need for additional time for teaching.

Herein lies one of the chief disadvantages in the subject-organization approach to elementary school curriculum development. In some instances subjects have been exalted and emphasized to the extent that some curriculums have become subject centered, with subjects being thought of as the end product rather than a means to the end. This implies that the emphasis should not be placed on the teaching of subjects but guiding, directing, and supervising behavior of children that results in learning.

Regardless of the situation indicated above, numerous teachers who are involved in the subject approach to elementary school curriculum organization are doing an outstanding job. Teachers who use the subject approach have two rather extreme alternatives to follow. They can teach for the sake of the subject in terms of merely imparting information, or they can be concerned with the needs and interests of children, and provide for desirable learning experiences for them in the various subject areas. If the latter course is taken, it is the responsibility of the teacher to assist children in understanding important relationships between subjects to the extent that various subjects may be drawn upon in the solution of problems. The extent to which teachers may accomplish this objective will be directly related to the prevailing philosophy of the local

---

[1]These areas should be considered as curriculums within the overall elementary school curriculum.

school administration with regard to the interpretation placed on the various subject-matter areas.

The Broad-Fields Version of Curriculum Development

It has been mentioned previously that one of the great dangers in the subject version of curriculum organization lies in the possibility that the curriculum could become overcrowded. As a safeguard against this contingency some school systems have followed a plan of curriculum organization that is based on certain broad fields.

When curriculum development is approached in this manner, it does not necessarily mean that certain subject-matter areas are entirely deleted, but rather that they may be included in a broad-fields area. For example, such individual subjects as history, geography, and civics might be incorporated into the broad area of social studies.

One of the major problems involved in organizing the elementary school curriculum on the broad-fields basis is that curriculum content must be developed in terms of broad concepts that are inherent in the various individual subjects that make up the broad area. This problem is further complicated by the fact that it may be difficult to develop the broad concepts and understandings over a range of grade levels. Although this procedure may be difficult to accomplish, the broad-fields approach offers the advantage of providing for a greater degree of latitude and flexibility. This implies that there are greater possibilities for capitalizing upon such factors as children's interests and community resources.

The Areas-of-living Approach to Curriculum Organization

The areas-of-living, or problems-of-living, approach concerns those life problems which confront children in our modern complex society. In educating for democracy it should certainly be a function of the school to develop basic understandings in democratic principles. In general, the areas-of-living approach focuses upon inherent problems in social situations and "getting along together." Due to this fact, this particular approach has been most prominent in the area of social studies.

An example of the areas-of-living approach is found in the case of a sixth-grade class that wished to improve existing condition in the school lunchroom. The problem was formulated with the guidance of the teacher, committees selected, and necessary procedures taken to solve the problem.

During the process of exploring the situation, the various committees gathered information and received help from numerous sources in the school and community. The committees presented their findings and recommendations for improvement and the result was an improved lunchroom—a problem in social living approached in true democratic fashion.

One of the major criticisms of the areas-of-living approach to curriculum organization at the elementary school level is that basic-skill teaching and learning are neglected. However, this may not be an entirely valid criticism in that the ability to perform certain skills will be necessary if problems are to be solved. Consequently, there is a distinct need for teaching the fundamental skills when the areas-of-living approach is employed. It should also be mentioned that in this approach the basic skills may be acquired as they are needed to solve problems. In this way children perhaps will be more likely to see the need for learning certain of the basic skills; whereas when they are taught skills independently of their use in solving problems of living, skill learning may be less tangible and consequently less meaningful to them.

The Needs Version of Curriculum Organization

The needs approach to curriculum organization means that learning experiences are provided in accordance with the needs of children. In order to carry out this version of curriculum organization, attempts should be made to analyze children's basic needs and then to provide satisfactory school experiences to help meet these needs.

Contrary to general opinion, the needs approach to curriculum organization is not a recent innovation. In fact, this plan probably had its inception in American elementary education in the early part of the 20th century when the Elementary School at the University of Missouri was established in 1904. History tells us[2] that this school "abandoned the conventional curriculum and developed methods of teaching required to make child needs and growth the dominant purpose of the school."

In considering children's needs as a basis for curriculum organization, demands of the culture must be taken into account. In this regard such factors as the requirements for social acceptance and the fluid character

---

[2]Thirteenth Yearbook of the John Dewey Society, *The American Elementary School*, ed. Harold G. Shane, New York, Harper & Brothers, 1953, p. 415.

of American culture might serve as guideposts for proper adjustment between cultural demands and the school curriculum. Not only must the demands of the culture be considered but also those of the child because these demands are indicated basically by the child's needs and interests. In other words, there should be (1) satisfaction of biological needs, (2) need for sense of personal achievement and personal worth, and (3) need for emotional security. It should be a function of the school to guide the learning of children so that these needs may be satisfied in acceptable ways.

The needs version of curriculum organization poses the problem of discovering satisfactory procedures for determining children's needs and what these needs imply for the curriculum. In this respect, although there may be some degree of general agreement that the elementary school curriculum should be based on the needs of children, at the same time there is some difference in opinion with regard to what the needs may be and what their implications are for the curriculum.

The commonly proposed needs of children represent a wide variety of usages of the term *needs* and suggest different courses of action on the part of the school. Because of this it might be well to analyze some of the different approaches in determining needs and resultant differences in conclusions.

A survey of the literature reveals that the determination of needs of children is a complex and varied problem, and an overview of the various conclusions reported could likely be more confusing than informing. Consequently, it seems essential here to examine the different approaches and resultant differences in conclusions.

The *inferential* or *rational* approach, based primarily on reflection of personal experiences with children, lacks objectivity. As such this approach is subject to the influences of the background of the person who had these experiences, his interests, and his purposes. Nevertheless, this approach has the advantage of avoiding the misinterpretations which may be placed on a mass of statistical data, and it allows also for analysis in the light of the broad background of an expert who has had years of experience in this specific area.

The *quantitative* approach is found most frequently in studies of person-adjustment problems, interests, and other concerns of children. The different results obtained usually depend upon the instruments used and the setting of the statements by individual authors.

The *statements of needs* formulated by groups have some advantage over statements of needs formulated by individuals in that some of the limitations of individual preparation, past experience, insight, and adjustments are countered by group judgments. However, the value of the statements of needs formulated by a group or an individual in the final analysis depends upon the abilities of the members of the group or the individual.

In consideration of the approaches that can be used in determining needs of children, it is suggested that the following lists of procedures might be valuable for determining needs of individual children and of the group.

Procedures Suggested as Valuable for Determining Needs of the Individual

1. Using an outline of needs to aid in understanding behavior.
2. Making use of the results of school medical examinations.
3. Using the results of physical education methods of classification.
4. Analysis of personal-adjustment needs.
5. Analysis of social-adjustments needs.
6. Analysis of recreation needs.

Procedures Suggested as Valuable for Determining Needs of the Group

1. Making use of the reports of studies of children.
2. Making one's own studies of children.
3. Making use of the reports of studies of the activities and problems of people in the community.
4. Making one's own studies of the activities and problems of people in the community.
5. Making use of the reports of studies of the activities and problems in our society.
6. Exploring the ideas of teachers regarding pupil needs.
7. Exploring the ideas of pupils regarding their needs.

It should be emphasized that the needs approach can be used for the following purposes:

1. To help teachers understand children.
2. To help children understand themselves.
3. To facilitate learning.
4. To help in reorganization of the curriculum.

5. To help in evaluation.
6. To help children help themselves.
7. To aid teachers in guiding children toward more effective living in a democracy.

Regardless of how needs are determined in a specific situation, it should be borne in mind that the needs version of curriculum organization can operate under varying circumstances in the elementary school. In other words, classroom activity can be carried on through units or through specific subject fields. The important factor is that the selection of activities will be based upon some type of analysis of children's needs.

ELEMENTARY SCHOOL CURRICULUM AREAS PROVIDED MOST FREQUENTLY ON A DAILY BASIS

The elementary school curriculum areas discussed here are those that appear to be offered most often on a day-to-day basis. As mentioned previously, and according to my extensive surveys, the basic three Rs are offered by practically all elementary schools. Also science and social studies, although not universally offered, are provided by a large majority of schools. (These are the curriculum areas considered for integration with physical education in Chapters 5 through 9).

READING

The ability to read was not considered important for most laymen until sometime after Johann Gutenberg invented the printing press in the 15th century, and the Protestant Reformation—with its emphasis on individual interpretation of the Bible. Until that time, reading was generally restricted to the clergy and certain members of the nobility.[3]

The Nature of Reading

To define exactly what reading means is not an easy task. A part of the reason for this is that it means different things to different people. It has been suggested that the psychologist thinks of reading as a thought process. Those who deal in semantics, which is the study of meanings, think of reading as the graphic representation of speech. The linguist,

---

[3]The New Columbia Encyclopedia, New York, Columbia University Press, 4th ed., 1975, p. 2284.

one who specializes in speech and language, is concerned with the sounds of language and its written form. Finally, the sociologist is concerned with the interaction of reading and culture.

Reading is an aspect of communication and as such, it becomes more than just being able to recognize a word on a printed page. To communicate, a meaning must be shared and the reader must be able to comprehend. Thus, one of the most important concerns in teaching reading is that of helping children develop comprehension skills.

Reading could be thought of as bringing meaning to the printed page instead of only gaining meaning *from* it. This means that the author of a reading selection does not necessarily convey ideas to the reader but stimulates him to construct them out of his own experience. (This is one of the major purposes of physical education reading content which will be dealt with in detail in a later Chapter.)

Since reading is such a complex act and it cannot be easily defined, I will resort to a rather broad and comprehensive description of the term. This description of reading is: *an interpretation of written or printed verbal symbols.* This can range from graffiti on restroom walls to the Harvard Classics.

It should be borne in mind that the entire child reads; he reads with his senses, his experiences, his cultural heritage, and of course with his muscles. It is the latter aspect with which the present author is predominantly concerned in this book because the aspect of "muscle sense" involved in physical education is an extremely important dimension in reading for children.

When to Begin Reading Instruction

Traditionally, the standard practice has been to begin the teaching of reading when children enter first grade at about six years of age. However, in recent years there appears to be a great deal of sentiment to start reading instruction before that time. A part of the reason for this is that there is a general feeling that young children are becoming more mature and possess more experience at an earlier age than was the case in the past. As a result of this prevailing belief, fully one-third of the teachers at the kindergarten level feel that their children can benefit from various forms of reading instruction. In fact, a large majority of kindergarten teachers conduct some of the fundamental phases of reading instruction, and only about 20 percent of these do *not* believe that reading instruction should be a part of the school program at that level.

A question that must be raised is: Does early reading instruction have any value? Completely solid evidence to support one position or another is lacking to make an unqualified valid conclusion. One very important consideration is whether or not early instruction benefits the child as far as his total development is concerned. Some child development specialists feel that such instruction, if too highly structured and formalized, can actually cause harm in some children as far as their emotional development and social adjustment are concerned.

It is important to mention at this point that education is as much the business of the home as of the school, because it is obvious that the school alone does not educate the child. Yet, many parents believe that a child begins to learn only when he enters school. They do not seem to realize that they are not only the child's first teacher but probably the most important one the child will ever have.

Parents can and should help prepare their children before they enter school and also assist their children with schoolwork after they are in school. An abundance of evidence is being accumulated to support this idea. For example, one national survey has shown that preschool children who have been "read to" by their parents perform better than those who do not receive such attention.

There are many valid reasons why this is true. Research in child development indicates that the direction of a child's mental development is likely to be determined between ten months and one and one-half years of age—and in some cases even lower. In addition, the human learning patterns can become well established by age three. Consequently, the action that parents take in helping their children is extremely important. Moreover, most authorities in the area of child development tend to feel that the first five years are the most important formative ones in the child's life. The child's ability to learn various skills in these formative years before he enters school may depend a good bit on the extent to which his parents provide him with desirable and worthwhile learning experiences.

It has been estimated that of the approximately three to four million children entering first grade, more than 400,000 of them will be asked to repeat that grade. It has been further estimated that if present trends continue, one-fourth of current first grade children, by the time they reach the age of 11 will be reading two or more years below grade level.

In fact, school officials of one large city system recently reported that about 50 percent of its students were dropping out of school at the ninth grade level because inability to read would prevent them from graduating from high school.

It is easy to blame the schools for this sad state of affairs. However, before doing so we might well take another look at the responsibility of parents as important helpers in the education of their children.

Reading Readiness

Closely allied to the problem of when to begin reading instruction is the question of reading readiness. There are certain *developmental tasks* that are important for children to accomplish. Reading can be considered as such a developmental task. That is, it is a task that a child needs to perform to satisfy his personal needs as well as those requirements which society and the culture impose upon him. In viewing reading as a developmental task, we can then consider reading readiness as a developmental *stage* at which certain factors have prepared the child for reading.

At one time, reading readiness was considered only as being concerned with the child being ready to *begin* the reading experience. In more recent years it has come to be thought of more in terms of each step of reading as one concerned with readiness for further reading. Therefore, the idea of reading readiness is not confined only to the start of reading instruction, but to the teaching and learning of most all reading skills. A given child may be considered ready to *learn to read* at a certain age. However, this same child may not necessarily be ready to *read to learn* until a later time. In fact, some reading specialists consider the primary level of grades one through three as a time for learning to read, and the intermediate level of grades four through six as a time when the child begins to read to learn.

Reading readiness needs to be thought of as a complex combination of basic abilities and conditions and not only as a single characteristic. This combination includes (1) various aspects of visual ability, (2) certain factors concerned with the auditory sense, (3) sex differences, (4) age, and (5) socioeconomic conditions. Obviously, it is not the purpose here to go into detail with reference to these various characteristics, but merely to identify them at this point. In Chapter 5 some specific recommendations will be made concerning the application and function of physical education as a medium for dealing with certain aspects of reading readiness.

WRITING

Almost all children want to write, and prior to starting school many children make an attempt. The child's desire to write most likely comes from his feeling that he can create something by scribbling on a piece of paper and from his wanting to imitate. Usually between the ages of three and four years the child makes marks for his name on birthday and Christmas cards to relatives and friends. From four to six years of age, he may try to write his name or copy a "thank-you" note that he has dictated to a parent or older sibling. At an early age children have been known, much to the alarm of some parents, to write on the walls to express themselves. Unfortunately, too many children are punished for this practice when they should be rewarded by being provided with writing materials to express themselves.

For the most part, children enter first grade with a desire to write. As the child develops and grows in his ability to express his thoughts and feelings well, he moves from writing one sentence "on his own" to writing many sentences involving length and structure and the organization of ideas into paragraphs.

It should be noted that merely providing opportunities to write will not necessarily mean that children will improve their writing. Direct guidance is needed by teachers. The important factors to consider are that (1) most all children want to write, and (2) they will perhaps write with originality, creativity, and spontaneity.

There is a natural relationship between writing and spelling. To learn to spell a word the child uses the same word recognition skills that he uses in reading. As the child writes, he spells the word he has heard (listening), has spoken (speaking), and has read (reading). These relationships make it much easier for the child to spell.

Handwriting involves physical coordination and manipulation. Thus, among other things, handwriting involves the use of muscles and bones of the hand and wrist. In addition, it is concerned with a high level of refinement between the hands and the eyes. As far as total language development is concerned, writing is preceded by listening, speaking, and reading. The child develops a listening vocabulary, and he will likely try to put into oral language the words he hears. Next, he may read about things that are of interest to him, and finally he will try to put into writing those things with which he is familiar.

For the above reason, it is the general opinion that *manuscript* writing may be best suited for children at the primary school level. In this type of writing all the letters of the alphabet are formed with straight lines and circles or parts of circles. The size of the writing tends to decrease with the child's development. Although the research in this area is inconclusive, the trend appears to be much in favor of manuscript for the beginners. Children who begin their writing experiences with manuscript seem to write more freely; they use a larger number of different words than do most children who begin with the *cursive* form. This form (cursive) requires the joining of letters into words, and it involves varying degrees of slanting. It is also interesting to note that children who begin their school experiences with manuscript seem to spell a larger number of words correctly than do children who begin with cursive writing. Ordinarily, as the child develops, cursive writing is introduced.

Writing Readiness

As was the case with reading readiness, children need to progress through certain developmental stages as far as writing readiness is concerned. There appears to be a marked relationship between maturity and writing readiness because, among other things, writing is dependent upon skill in movement, manual dexterity, and eye-hand coordination. Movements of the eyes tend to develop sooner than the more refined finger movements. Therefore, the former will guide the writing hand as the child begins to write. At a later time both of these movements become coordinated to the extent that writing becomes more or less an automatic process.

An important writing readiness factor to keep in mind is that it is a common characteristic for children to reverse letters, such as writing *d* for *b*. This is likely due to the limited development of eye-hand coordination previously mentioned, and it can be expected to occur in children at five or six years of age. In fact, immature development in eye-hand coordination may continue in some children until they are well beyond six years of age.

Alert teachers are sensitive to the importance of writing readiness skills at the outset of the writing program when a child enters school.

MATHEMATICS

The subject of mathematics in today's elementary schools, with the never-ending attempts at new methods and changes in content, is understandably bewildering to the conscientious teacher who must encounter every new and different procedure.

Over the years there have been many periods of change in mathematics in schools, and believe it or not, there was a time when mathematics was not even considered a proper subject of study for children. In the very early days of this country the ability to compute was regarded as appropriate for a person doing menial work, but such skill was not viewed as appropriate for the aristocracy. Accordingly the study of mathematics was not emphasized in the early schools of America, not event the study of arithmetic.[4]

Gradually, as commerce increased, the ability to compute became increasingly valued and arithmetic became a part of the general education of the young, gaining an equal place in the curriculum with religion, reading, and writing. Late in the 18th century, laws to make arithmetic a mandatory school subject were passed in Massachusetts and New Hampshire. During this period, arithmetic was used primarily by businessmen and very gradually came into the schools of the day, and by 1800 arithmetic was taught quite generally in the schools.

Arithmetic, as taught during the early decades of the new nation, consisted of working problems from rules. Only the teacher had a book, and the rules presented were applied largely to problems of commerce of that day. Arithmetic was seldom taught to children below ten years of age, and, in fact, when a boy started to study the subject, it was considered as sign of approaching manhood.

Mathematics has been, and continues to be, viewed by large numbers of children as something to be dreaded, for in the early stages exercises were deliberately designed to be difficult in order to "exercise" the mind. Examples of written problems provided for children include the following:

What is the cost of 9¼ tons of coal, if .875 of a ton costs $5.635?

Bought 6/7 of a box of candles, and having used 7/8 of them, sold the

---

[4]In the early 1960s the subject of arithmetic became more generally known as "elementary school mathematics." No doubt the reason for this was that at about this time elementary schools were beginning to include more advanced forms of mathematical processes in addition to the traditional study of arithmetic, which is considered to be a branch of the broader area of mathematics.

remainder for ¹⁶/₂₅ of a dollar; how much would a box cost at the same rate?

It was thought that such problems would help children think clearly and quickly. It is questionable whether today's instruction in mathematics has as yet completely recovered from the accompanying dread of arithmetic and the idea that "difficult is good" and "fun must be bad."

As time went on there was more of an effort to restrict problems in arithmetic to those encountered in the normal daily lives of the adult population. It was felt in general that the school should think of arithmetic somewhat beyond the needs of adults. This procedure, known as the *social utility theory* was greatly extended as research on the actual use of arithmetic began. Some of the advocates of social utility theory believed that with the program simplified results should be much better and 100 percent mastery of the fundamentals should be expected.

The emphasis on social utility resulted in the development of problem units for different grades. For example, "grocery store at school" in Grade Two. "The home garden, does it pay?" in Grade Four, and so on. Children studying arithmetic under the influence of social utility theory were not usually without drill exercises in the course of their progress through the grades, but arithmetic *was* understood to be something that would be used, and instruction often involved more informal child participation. (It is interesting to note that it was about this time—the late 1930s—that the use of games to teach arithmetic began to be encouraged. However, for the most part these games were passive in nature and not necessarily those kinds of physical education experiences that I advocate in Chapter 6, which are based on a total or near-total physical response of the child.)

Before long, drill came to be emphasized less, for it was thought that mastery required less drill if learning occurred in a meaningful situation; thus, there came into being the *meaning theory*. This meant that there was a movement away from stressing only social meanings towards more of a stress on mathematical meanings. The term *meaning theory* is commonly associated with this movement, which had considerable impact on instruction in the 1940s and 1950s. It was reasoned that stress on socially useful arithmetic had too often been accompanied with rote instruction on the fundamentals and by drill, which made little mathematical sense to the child. Educators who promoted meaning theory stressed the need for helping children *understand* processes, and they taught that drill was to be used only to reinforce material the child already understood.

Over the years, the word meaningful has been used in so many different ways that confusion has understandably resulted. When the term is used to refer to instruction in which the mathematics makes sense to the child; that is, when he understands *why*, then it is appropriate to contrast meaningful instruction with rote instruction. However, since the 1930s meaningful instruction has often been contrasted with drill or practice. As a result, dangerously little practice has been included in some programs.

Changes in elementary school mathematics programs since the mid-1950s have been rather dramatic. These changes can be viewed as an acceleration of the changes toward more mathematically meaningful instruction that had taken place during the previous two decades, perhaps with a change in focus. Several factors converged to help bring about the "revolution" that occurred.

First of all, mathematics itself had changed, and attempts to unify mathematical concepts led to new basic structures that had not yet been reflected in mathematics instruction below the university level. Another contributing factor was the accumulating information about how children learn, for it was becoming well established that children could learn quite complex concepts, often at a younger age. Other factors often cited include the concern that the mathematics curriculum was largely the result of historical development rather than logical development, the increasing need for an understanding of mathematics by people in business and industry, and a belief on the part of many people that there was an overemphasis on computational skills.

The elementary school mathematics programs that were developed during the late 1950s and the 1960s focused heavily upon concepts and principles and became immediately known as the *new math*. The content of programs for elementary school children contained more algebraic ideas and more geometry than had been included in previous years. In addition, such things as relationships between operations were stressed.

When the *new math* was introduced into the American educational system it was probably one of the greatest upheavals in curriculum content and procedures in modern times. It also became the victim of much ridicule by educators and laymen alike. One night club entertainer was prompted to describe the purpose of the *new math* as "to get the idea, *rather* than the right answer." One of my own mathematician friends, in comparing the *old math* and the *new math,* inferred that in the *old math* "they knew how to do it but didn't know what they were doing;" whereas in the *new math,* "they know what they are doing but they don't know how to do it."

In general, the *new math* was intended to do away with a process that had focused upon rote memory and meaningful computation. Further, it was expected that the new process would make it easier for students to develop mathematical understandings. The extent to which the *new math* achieved success has been challenged by some. Obviously, most educational innovations have rightly been criticized when one gives consideration to the extremes that are possible in any educational process. Because of this, it now appears that attempts are being made to reach some sort of happy medium. While it is not likely that anyone wishes to revert entirely to the *old math,* at the same time, it would be desirable to avoid some of the extremes that have brought harsh criticism of the *new math.*

At the present time this seems to be the prevailing notion among many mathematics educators. It appears that present approaches to mathematics programs for children are such that they are being directed toward situations that are more suited to the everyday facts of life. It is the premise of the present author that the physical education approach to learning about mathematics not only deals with the everyday facts of life, *but with life itself* — at least as far as the child is concerned.

SCIENCE

During the past several decades the science program in the elementary school has been characterized by widely divergent practices. In the early years of the 19th century, what passed for science in the early common schools consisted of certain *wonders of the supernatural.* This is to say that teachers were expected to convey information to children that might help them to appreciate the various aspects of nature. Children were not expected to understand that there were natural causes for certain things that happened, but rather to believe that some mysterious application of a higher power was enough of an explanation for things that occurred.

Later on an instructional procedure known as *object teaching* was introduced. The purpose of this approach as far as science was concerned, was for children to observe certain objects under the detailed directions given by the teacher. Children were expected to memorize various details about these objects. Properties of the objects were observed in a sequence with little or no regard as to how one particular object might be related to another. Perhaps the reason for this was that in those days the belief was still held that children were not able to understand such relationships. Of all of the weaknesses of such an approach, it had at least one aspect to commend it. This was that in object teaching, the actual objects studied needed to be available for the children to see and manipulate.

Eventually, object teaching was replaced by *nature study;* this aspect of science in elementary education continued for about a half century. A part of the basis for this has been attributed to the notion that there was a desire to improve the lagging agricultural economy and to prevent the accumulation of unemployed rural migrants in the city.

In actual practice the nature study approach did not differ appreciably from object teaching. It appeared that the basic idea of nature study was to help children develop an understanding and life-long appreciation of nature. The extent to which this was accomplished has been open to question, but nevertheless the practice continued until shortly after World War I.

In the mid 1920s a newer concept of science education was introduced into many elementary schools of America. This approach was referred to as the doctrine of social utility. This meant generally that science should be considered in terms of its practical application in solving certain problems that had to be encountered in daily living. It is interesting to note that in a number of instances this approach is in effect at the present time, although it is being subjected to continuing criticism.

The transition of methods and content in any subject area is not likely to be characterized by sharp lines of demarcation. Such is the case with elementary school science because the transition from the doctrine of social utility has been occurring over a period of years and in fact in some cases is still in the process. One of the highlights in this transition period occurred in the late 1940s when action was taken by the National Council for the Study of Education.[5] The Forty-Sixth Yearbook of the Council stated that children should by the end of each year have experienced growth in the broader areas of *physical* and *biological* environment such as the following: (1) The Universe, (2) The Earth, (3) Conditions

---

[5]National Society for the Study of Education, *Forty-Sixth Yearbook*, Part I, Science Education in American Schools, Chicago, University of Chicago Press, 1947, pp. 75–76.

Necessary for Life, (4) Living Things, (5) Physical and Chemical Changes Phenomena, and (6) Man's Attempt to Control His Environment.

In the early 1950s, experts in the area of elementary school science were advocating a shift away from the type of curriculum offering that was based merely on satisfying curiosity, and suggesting that the trend should be in the direction of providing learning experiences in science that were of real concern in the lives of children.

Perhaps the greatest single incident which provided the most impact for science education at all educational levels in America was the occasion of the Soviet Union's launching of the *sputnik* in October 1957. As a result of this, unprecedented interest was generated in science in the elementary school, and responsible groups and individuals were spurred to action to improve curriculum offerings.

Current Practices in Elementary School Science

Despite the fact that a major effort has been made to initiate changes in the elementary school science curriculum, implementation as far as various curriculum projects is concerned has not been extensive. Possibly the primary reason for this is the apprehension that there may develop a trend toward a national curriculum in science.

As in the case of many other curriculum areas in the elementary school, local school systems tend to provide for their own specific science curriculum. These, of course, range from poor to outstanding programs, depending upon the available natural corollaries needed for success in such programs.

A constant characteristic of most local programs is that they tend to arrive at some sort of scope and sequence which best meet the needs at the local level. Scope is concerned with the science learning experiences to be provided (concepts to be developed), and sequence refers to the grade placement of such experiences. There is a relatively high degree of agreement as to the major areas of study for science, but agreement is not necessarily found as far as sequence is concerned.

It is also interesting to note that there are a variety of ways which are used to organize and provide for science learning experiences in the elementary school. In general, these include (1) science as a separate subject, (2) separate sciences units, (3) utilizing science opportunities when they occur, and (4) incorporating science experiences in large units of study, as in the social studies.

SOCIAL STUDIES

For many years such subjects as history, geography, civics, and the like have been included among the curriculum offerings of the elementary school. In the traditional elementary school these subjects were dealt with as more or less isolated and separate entities in which the child was expected to master an abundance of facts.

The term *social studies* was officially adopted as the name of a curriculum area in 1916 by the Committee on Social Studies of the Commission on the Reorganization of Secondary Education of the National Education Association.

Throughout this century the social studies has been linked to the idea of citizenship education. The National Council for the Social Studies, the principal professional organization for social studies teachers, has stated that "the basic goal of social studies education is to prepare young people to be humane, rational, participating citizens in a world that is becoming increasingly interdependent."[6] According to the National Council, this goal can be achieved by having students attain certain knowledge, abilities, and values, and by involving them in social participation.

The term *social studies* has been employed to denote a broad area of study which would ordinarily comprise curriculum content contained in such separate subjects as history, geography, and civics. (In some cases it has been extended to include science and health and safety as well.) However, merely combining these subjects into an area referred to as social studies does not necessarily ensure that children will be provided with satisfactory learning experiences in social relationships commensurate with their needs in modern society.

Perhaps one of the most recent authoritative statements concerning tendencies in elementary school social studies appeared in the *Eightieth Yearbook of the National Society for the Study of Education* in 1981.[7] It was proposed that at the elementary school level, we may anticipate a renaissance of interest in using social studies as the integrating center of the school curriculum. Three reasons were advanced to support this contention: First, there is simply not enough time to accomodate all the sepa-

_____

[6]National Council for the Social Studies, *Revision of the NCSS Social Studies Curriculum Guidelines,* Washington, DC, The Council, 1979, p. 1.

[7]Jarolimek, J., The social studies: An overview, Eightieth Yearbook of the National Society for the Study of Education, Chicago, University of Chicago Press, 1981, pp 15–16.

rate demands made of the curriculum. Each year new topics or concerns encroach on a fixed amount of instructional time. Thus, elementary schools must either stop doing something they now do in order to make time for new thrusts, or they must become more efficient in the way they conduct their programs. One way of using the available time more productively is to combine some of the curriculum components. Because elementary schools are committed to self-contained classrooms, combining subjects is both sensible and possible.

Second, the elementary school curriculum is badly fragmented with subjects and topics and needs some type of organizing, integrating framework. Social studies units of study are an appropriate way to provide such organization. Moreover, an integrated instructional program can provide a good balance between process outcomes and substantive learnings. As children work toward the attainment of social studies knowledge goals, they can read, write reports and stories, speak and listen to others, and participate in art, music, and dramatic activities.

Third, social studies enables children to acquire important skills in a *functional* situation. Children do not read and write outside of some subject matter context; that is, they read and write about some subject or topic. Much of what they read and write about could be related to the on-going social studies program. Much good skill instruction in reading, writing, spelling, arithmetic, and speaking can be accomplished through social studies. The reverse is also true. Rather than detracting from the elementary school's concern for teaching basic skills, social studies education, if properly handled, can greatly enhance the teaching of such skills.

Despite the above optimistic pronouncements it is interesting to note that recently there has been a call from some critics to return to more traditional separate subjects offerings in the areas of geography and history. The major reason for this is that some very recent surveys have indicated that many college students cannot identify certain locations on a map, and also that they are completely unaware of certain important historical dates.

In this general connection, it should be mentioned that the 41st president of the United States in a campaign address to a group of military veterans on September 7, 1988 proclaimed that date as Pearl Harbor Day. Interestingly enough, and indeed unfortunately, this gaffe was passed off by some as more or less of a joke with one "political pundit" suggesting that "he only missed the date by three months."

THE FUTURE OF ELEMENTARY SCHOOL CURRICULUM DEVELOPMENT

Although it may be hazardous to speculate on the future status of the elementary school curriculum, it seems safe to make a few generalizations based upon the way in which the past has challenged the present and how the present might challenge the future.

It is hoped that in general, improvement in curriculum organization might be expected in the future, with more elementary schools benefiting from such improvement. Although it could be wishful thinking, this assumption is based on the idea that in a democracy, that which is best and needed most by the majority of the people will prevail.

It is extremely difficult to visualize how complex the social and cultural problems will be for future generations. However, it would appear that the elementary school curriculum should be able to keep pace with social needs by employing procedures that are based upon meeting a proper balance between the demands of the culture and demands of the child. This implies that with a changing culture the elementary school curriculum must not be allowed to remain static. Therefore, elementary school curriculums of the future are likely to receive a great deal more attention with regard to continuous development based on scientific principles of evaluation in order to meet the needs of an ever rapidly changing society.

Chapter 2

PHYSICAL EDUCATION
IN THE ELEMENTARY SCHOOL

HISTORICAL DEVELOPMENT AND CURRENT TRENDS

In order to present a clearer picture of the place of physical education in the modern elementary school, it seems appropriate to discuss briefly its past development. Moreover, if we can see how the past has challenged the present, there is a strong likelihood that we may be able to understand more fully how the present might challenge the future.

There is a widespread notion among some people at the present time that physical education at the elementary school level is something new. This idea is probably prompted by the fact that physical education at this level has been receiving more attention in recent years and by the additional fact that more emphasis is being put on it in some school systems.

Contrary to this general belief, physical education at the elementary school level is not of recent origin. In fact, educators and philosophers as far back as the early Greeks felt that physical education activities might be a welcome adjunct to the total education of children. For instance, over 2,300 years ago Plato suggested that all early education should be a sort of play and develop around play situations.

In the 17th century, Locke, the English philosopher felt that children should get plenty of exercise and learn to swim early in life. Rousseau, the notable French writer, held much the same opinion, believing that learning should develop from the activities of childhood. These men, along with numerous others, influenced to some extent the path that elementary school physical education was to follow through the years.

Throughout the ages physical education programs have been caught between mere preparation of the body for combat and a recognition of the essential unity of the mind and body in the educative process. In addition, there have been periods when any type of physical education program was abandoned purely on the basis that body pleasure of any sort must be subjugated because it was associated with evil doing. The early American pioneers more or less typified this kind of puritanical thinking because there was no emphasis on physical education for the pioneer child as far as formal education was concerned. Although physical education received no attention in the early American schools, a series of factors over a period of a few years were instrumental in effecting a radical change, such as Western expansion, wars, application of inventions which revolutionized travel and communications, and the concentration of population, all having an influence on the growth of the early common schools. Although the early grade schools in the mid-19th century were concerned predominantly with the academic subject matter of reading, writing, and arithmetic, the need for physical activity as a part of the school day was becoming evident. As a result, some time for physical exercise was allotted in the school programs of Boston as early as 1852. St. Louis and Cincinnati followed this procedure in 1855 and 1859 respectively. Interest at the state level began to appear and a state law requiring physical education was passed in California in 1866. The fact that the public was becoming conscious of the play needs of children was indicated by the establishment of the first playground in Boston in 1885.

In 1889 in that same city an interesting development occurred at a "conference in the interest of physical training." School administrators were beginning to feel the pressure and need for some kind of formal physical activity as a genuine part of the school program. Acting in a conservative manner at this conference, some school administrators proposed that a "physical training" program might be introduced as a part of the school day, but that it must consume only a short period of time, minimal expenditure of money, and take place in the classroom. The Swedish pedogogical system of gymnastics, which was designed to systematically exercise the entire body in a single lesson, was proposed since this system satisfactorily met the criteria established by the school administrators. On June 24, 1890, the Boston School Committee voted that this system of gymnastics be introduced in all of the public schools of Boston. Although this proposal was a far cry from a well-balanced elementary physical education program as we understand it today, it nevertheless served as a formal introduction of organized physical activity into the elementary school on the recommendation of school administrators. It should be mentioned, however, that the main objective of physical education in the eyes of school administrators of that day was that it should serve as a release for prolonged periods of mental fatigue. It was believed the main purpose of engaging in physical activity was to provide children with a "break" in the school day so that they would approach their studies more vigorously.

This condition existed until such time that there was more widespread acceptance of the theory of mind-body relationship and the education of the *whole* person. John Dewey, one of the early believers in this principle, introduced the concept of a balanced physical education program while at the University of Chicago Laboratory School early in this century. Rather than only the more or less formalized gymnastics program, this school began to include games and dancing as a part of the physical education experiences for children. Some years later Dewey commented that "Experience has shown that when children have a chance at physical activities which bring their natural impulses into play, going to school is a joy, management is less of a burden, and learning is easier.[1]

However, up until the First World War physical education programs for elementary school children, where they did exist, consisted mainly of the formalized gymnastics and/or exercise types of programs. The period between the two world wars saw more attempts at balancing physical education programs at the elementary school level with more emphasis being placed upon games and rhythmic activities.

After World War II a number of factors developed which were to bring attention to the importance of physical education for young children. One estimate indicated that from the period of 1945 to 1955 more published material appeared relating to elementary school physical education than was the case in the preceding 50 years. In addition, many areas of the country began to provide elementary school physical education workshops and other in-service education devices for elementary school personnel. In 1948, at its annual convention, the American Association for Health, Physical Education and Recreation inaugurated an Elementary School Physical Education Section with the present author as its first chairman-elect. And in 1951 the first National Conference on Physical Education for Children of Elementary School Age was held in Washington, DC. (The term *Association* has been changed to *Alliance* in this national organization.)

The period from 1950 to 1975 saw a continuation of the foundation

---

[1]Dewey, John, *Democracy and Education, An Introduction to Philosophy of Education,* New York, Macmillan, 1919, pp. 228–229.

that had been laid in the preceding years. Numerous national conferences, the appointment of an Elementary School Consultant by the Alliance, and upgrading of teacher preparation in the area of elementary school physical education have been important factors. The more or less recent "discovery" of the importance of *movement* in the lives of children has contributed to better elementary school physical education programs in the decade of the 1980s and until the present time.

Speaking of movement, it seems appropriate at this point to comment on what has been called *movement education.* It is the belief of most physical educators that *movement* is the term which is most characteristic of the body of knowledge and subject matter in physical education. A common description of movement, when it applies to human beings, is muscular action involving a change in body position. The human organism interacts with its environment through changes in the position of the body and/or its segments through movement.

It is difficult to fix an exact date when the term *movement education* was introduced into the United States. However, it appears that this area was beginning to become known in this country in the mid-1950s, although it was a few years later before there was much widespread interest in it in the elementary schools. Many people feel that movement education originated in England but there are some who contend that the way that it has been conducted is a product of the thinking of American physical educators.

One of the problems encountered in movement education has been the difficulty of understanding its meaning. So many different definitions of it have been set forth in the literature that widespread confusion about the meaning of it has resulted.

Perhaps a generalized view would describe it as the *development of total human movement potential.* In movement education this is said to be accomplished by giving children freedom to explore various forms of movement with reference to such qualities as *time, force, space,* and *flow.* A brief comment on each of these qualities follows.

1. *Time.* Time is concerned with how long it takes to complete a movement. For example, a movement can be slow and deliberate such as a child attempting to create his own body movement to depict a falling snowflake. On the other hand, a movement might be made with sudden quickness such as starting to run for a goal on a signal.

2. *Force*. Force needs to be applied to set the body or one of its segments in motion as well as to change its speed and/or direction. Thus, force is concerned with how much strength is required for movement. Swinging an arm requires less strength than attempting to propel the body over the surface area with a standing broad jump.

3. *Space*. In general, there are two factors concerned with space. These are the amount of space required to perform a particular movement and the utilization of space available.

4. *Flow*. All movements involve some degree of rhythm in their performance; thus, flow is concerned with the sequence of movement involving rhythmic motion.

The above factors are included in all body movements in various degrees. The degree to which each is used effectively in combination will determine the extent to which the movement is performed with skill. As mentioned previously, the area of movement education purports to give children freedom in exploring various forms of movement with reference to the above qualities.

In 1980 I conducted a national survey regarding trends in movement education and some interesting information was revealed. In approximately 45 percent of the cases the movement education "approach" was gaining in popularity whereas in 37 percent of the cases it was declining. In 18 percent of the cases interest in the approach appeared to be remaining the same. Interest in this approach appears to have begun about the mid-1960s, reaching a peak about 1970. In some parts of the country this interest has been maintained while in others it has waned. General reasons give for the gain in popularity include (1) it is an important part of a balanced program for the primary level, (2) it helps children become more aware of their bodies, and (3) there is an interest in all aspects of elementary school physical education. Reasons given for a decline in popularity were (1) it overlooks the planned approach with instruction in various motor skill techniques, (2) traditional teachers will not subscribe to it, and (3) there is too much confusion about it as teachers do not understand the purpose of it.

In general, it appears that interest in the movement education approach has leveled off at least to a certain extent. In some cases physical educators divided into "camps" with respect to what some have referred to as the "traditional" approach as compared to the "movement education approach." This is most unfortunate because we should be working in the direction of what is in the best interest of children.

It is interesting to note that there is little research to support either approach unequivocally when used in the extreme. What little evidence is available suggests that a combination of the so-called traditional approach and the so-called movement education approach may be the most beneficial in teaching physical education activities to elementary school children.

Certainly any approach that is taken in our dealings with children as far as movement experiences are concerned should first and foremost take into account how well their needs are being met, along with procedures which are compatible with what we know about the learning process and how children learn.

It should appear evident from this short historical background that elementary school physical education has traveled a strange and sometimes hazardous road in reaching the level of importance that is attributed to it in modern education. However, in spite of the various pitfalls this area of education in the elementary school has forged ahead to the point where there has been almost unbelievable and unparalled progress in the past few years. This does not mean that the proponents for this area of education can become lethargic. Much needs to be done to continue to interpret the place and function of physical education in the modern elementary school curriculum, as well as to provide ways and means whereby physical education learning experiences can become even more valuable in the total growth and development of the elementary school child.

SOME CONCEPTS OF CHILD DEVELOPMENT AND THEIR MEANING FOR PHYSICAL EDUCATION

There has been a great deal of observation and research dealing with the growth and development of children. This information is most important to teachers in that it provides them with an understanding of how children might grow and develop in a way that is appropriate to their innate capacities and the environment in modern society.

Child development specialists have formulated what are termed concepts of physical, social, emotional, and intellectual development. A few examples of some of these are given here together with suggestions of their meaning for physical education. (It should be understood that only a partial list of these concepts is submitted and that the interested reader can resort to appropriate sources for a more detailed listing.)

Concepts of Physical Development

Physical Development and Change Are Continuous

In the early years physical education programs might well be characterized by large muscle activities. As the child develops, more difficult types of skills and activities can be introduced so that physical education experiences progress in a way that is compatible with the child's development.

Physical Development is Controlled by Both Heredity and Environment

The physical education program should be planned in a way to meet the innate capacities of each child. The teacher should attempt to establish an environmental climate where all children have an equal opportunity for wholesome participation.

Differences in Physical Development Occur at Each Age Level

This implies that there should be a wide variety of activities to meet the needs of children at various developmental levels. While gearing activities to meet the needs of a particular group of children the teacher should also attempt to provide for individual differences of children within the group.

Sex Differences in Development Occur at Different Ages

At the early levels of the elementary school, perhaps in grades one and two, boys and girls can participate satisfactorily together in most activities. As sex differences involving such factors as strength and endurance occur, provision might well be made for the separation of boys and girls in certain types of activities.

Needs of a Physical Nature Must be Satisfied if a Child Is to Function Effectively

Physical education lessons should be planned to provide an adequate activity yield. At the same time the teacher should be aware of fatigue symptoms so that children are not likely to go beyond their physical capacity. Physical education programs should be vigorous enough to meet the physical needs of children and at the same time motivating enough so that they will desire to perpetuate the physical education experience outside of the school.

Concepts of Social Development

Man is a Social Being

Opportunities should be provided for children to experience followership as well as leadership. The teacher should capitalize upon the social skills that are inherent in most physical education activities.

Interpersonal Relationships Have Social Needs as Their Basis

All children should be given an equal opportunity in physical education participation. Moreover, the teacher should impress upon children their importance to the group. This can be done in connection with the team or group effort that is essential to successful participation.

A Child Can Develop His Self-Concept Through Undertaking Roles

A child is more likely to be aware of his particular abilities if he is given the opportunity to play the different positions in a team game. Rotation of such responsibilities as squad or group leaders tends to provide opportunity for self-expression of children through role playing.

There Are Various Degrees of Interaction Between Individuals and Groups

Physical education provides a potentially excellent setting for the child to develop interpersonal interaction. The teacher has an opportunity to observe the children in a movement situation rather than in only a sedentary situation; consequently, he or she is in a good position to guide integrative experiences by helping children see the importance of satisfactory interrelationships in physical education group situations.

Choosing and Being Chosen, an Expression of a Basic Need, is a Foundation of Interpersonal Relationships

As far as possible, children should be given the responsibility for choosing teammates, partners, and the like. However, great caution should be taken by the teacher to see that this is carried out in an equitable way. The teacher should devise ways of choice so that certain children are not always selected last or left out entirely.

Concepts of Emotional Development

An Emotional Response May be Brought About by a Goal's Being Furthered or Thwarted

The teacher should make a very serious effort to assure successful experience for every child in his physical education activities. This can be accomplished in part by attempting to provide for individual differences within given physical education activities. The physical education setting should be such that each child derives a feeling of personal worth through making some sort of positive contribution.

Self-Realization Experiences Should Be Constructive

The opportunity for creative experience inherent in many physical education activities affords the child an excellent change for self-realization through physical expression. Teachers might well consider planning with children to see that activities are meeting their needs and as a result involve a constructive experience.

As the Child Develops, His Emotional Reactions Tend to Become Less Violent and More Discriminating

A well-planned program and progressive sequence of physical education activities can provide for release of aggression in a socially acceptable manner.

Depending on Certain Factors, a Child's Own Feelings May be Accepted or Rejected by the Individual

The child's physical education experience should make him feel good and have confidence in himself. Satisfactory self-concept seems closely related to body control; therefore, physical education experiences might be considered as one of the best ways of contributing to it.

Concepts of Intellectual Development

Children Differ in Intelligence

Teachers should be aware that poor performance of some children in physical education activities might be due to the fact that they have not understood the directions. Differences in intelligence levels as well as in physical skill and ability need to be taken into account in the planning of physical education lessons.

Mental Development Is Rapid in Early Childhood and Slows Down Later

Children want and need challenging kinds of physical education experiences. Physical education lessons should be planned and taught in much the same way as other curriculum areas of the elementary school. This precludes a program that is devoted entirely to what has been called "nondirected play."

Intelligence Develops Through the Interaction of the Child and His Environment

Movement experiences in physical education involve a process of interacting with the environment. There are many problem-solving opportunities in the well-planned physical education environment and hence the child can be presented with challenging learning situations.

Situations Which Encourage Total Personality Development Appear to Provide the Best Situation for Intellectual Development

The potential for total personality development (physical, social, emotional, and intellectual) is more evident in physical education than in any other single curriculum area in the elementary school. If one were to analyze each of the curriculum areas for its potentialities for physical, social, emotional, and intellectual development, it is doubtful that any one of these areas would compare with the potential that is inherent in the physical education learning situation.

OBJECTIVES OF PHYSICAL EDUCATION

It should be readily discerned that the component elements of total development become the objectives of physical education in the elementary school. These elements have been expressed in terms of physical, social, emotional, and intellectual development of children of elementary school age, and as such become the physical, social, emotional, and intellectual objectives of elementary school physical education.

The Physical Objective

This objective should imply the development of skill and ability in a variety of physical education activities together with organic development commensurate with vigor, vitality, strength, balance, flexibility, and neuromuscular coordination.

The Social Objective

This objective should imply satisfactory experiences in how to meet and get along with others, development of proper attitudes toward one's peers, and the development of a sense of values.

The Emotional Objective

This objective should imply that sympathetic guidance should be provided in meeting anxieties, joys, and sorrows, and help given in developing aspirations, affections, and security.

The Intellectual Objective

This objective should imply the development of specific knowledge pertaining to rules, regulations, and strategies involved in a variety of worthwhile physical education learning experiences. It addition, this objective should be concerned with the value of physical education as a most worthwhile learning medium in the development of concepts and understandings in other curriculum areas—the major concern of this book!

CONSIDERATIONS IN PLANNING PHYSICAL EDUCATION EXPERIENCES

Every school experience should contribute to the growth and development of children. If physical education is to play its part in meeting the goals of education, it must be carefully planned to meet the developmental needs of children at each grade level.

If you remember the objectives just discussed you are ready to take the first step in planning for desirable and worthwhile physical education experiences for children. That is, you are able to state clearly what you hope to accomplish in physical education. The second step is to determine what physical education experiences should be provided so that the objectives can be reached.

However, there is a third essential consideration to take into account. Although the ultimate objectives are the same for all grade levels the *means* used to achieve these objectives are different in certain ways. This is to say that the physical education experiences provided in the primary grades should differ from those offered in the intermediate grades. The children in grades kindergarten through grade three are different, developmentally speaking, from those in grades four through six. Children in each stage of the developmental process have their unique characteristics. An important aspect of program planning is that which is concerned with the selection of physical education activities that are compatible with the developmental level of the children to be taught. The important thing is to understand the basic concept of adjusting physical education experiences to meet the changing needs, interests, and abilities of children as they grow and develop.

Let us use mathematics to illustrate how another curriculum area is adjusted to the mental development of children as they progress through the grades. Simple number concepts are developed in the primary grades such as counting and understanding numbers and numeration systems. The progression for learning the various operations in arithmetic begins with addition, the least difficult, and proceeds through the more difficult operations of subtraction, multiplication, and division.

Virtually everyone accepts this progression of skills from the least difficult to the more difficult in mathematics, reading, the development of science concepts and the like. Far fewer people realize that the need for such progression is just as great in physical education. On average, the primary school age child is simply not ready for highly complex games like football. It is, of course, true that we occasionally find some children who have unusual talent in some sport. There are also child geniuses in mathematics, music, and art, but no one claims that elementary school offerings for *all* children should be adjusted to the very small number of children who are exceptional in ability.

Qualified physical educators recognize that if activities are misplaced in the physical education curriculum, they may lose their value and may even detract from rather than contribute to optimum growth and development of children. For this reason great care must be exercised in the proper selection of physical education curriculum content.

ELEMENTARY SCHOOL
PHYSICAL EDUCATION CURRICULUM CONTENT

Generally speaking, there are three broad categories of physical education activities which help to meet certain recognized needs of elementary school children. These categories involve (1) active games, (2) rhythmic activities, and (3) self-testing activities. Although these categories remain much the same for all the grade levels, the complexity of activities within each category increases. There is still another category which is involved in all of the above and this is the area of *basic movement and fundamental skills.* Being able to move effectively and efficiently is directly related to the proficiency with which the child will be able to perform the various fundamental motor skills. In turn, the success children will have in physical education activities will be dependent upon their proficiency of performance of these skills.

Basic Movement and Fundamental Skills

Just as the perception of symbols is concerned with reading readiness, so is basic movement an important factor in readiness to perform in various kinds of physical education activities. Since proficient performance of physical education activities is dependent upon skill of body movement, the ability of the child to move effectively should be readily discerned. This could be an important function of the area previously described as movement education. Some authorities in movement education subscribe to this notion by maintaining that sometimes at a very early age a child may discover and use combinations of movements which in reality are — or will eventuate into — specialized motor skills normally used in the complex organization of a game or dance.

In this sense, the child is becoming ready for direct skill teaching and learning. With proper teacher guidance the basic movements that he has developed on his own can be improved in terms of proper principles of body mechanics and commensurate with his natural ability. The important factor is that in the early stages the child has been made to feel comfortable with the way he moves and thus is in a better position to learn correct performance of skills.

These skills involve (1) the locomotor skills of walking, running, leaping, jumping, hopping, galloping, skipping, and sliding; (2) the auxiliary skills of starting, stopping, dodging, pivoting, landing, and falling; and (3) the skills of propulsion and retrieval such as throwing, striking, kicking, and catching.

Active Games

For purposes here games are described as *active interactions of individuals in competitive and/or cooperative situations.* This description of games places emphasis on *active* games as opposed to those that are *passive* in nature. This is to say that games in physical education are concerned with a total or near total physical response of children as they interact with each other.

In general, games played in small groups are enjoyed by most children at the primary level. These games ordinarily involve a few simple rules and in some cases elementary strategy. Games that involve chasing and fleeing, tag, and one small group against another, as well, as those involving fundamental skills, are best suited to children at the lower elementary levels. In addition, children at this age level enjoy the game with an element of surprise, such as those that involve running for a goal on a given signal.

Children in the intermediate level retain an interest in some of the games they played at the primary level, and some of them can be extended and made more difficult to meet the needs and interests of these older children. In addition, games may now be introduced that call for greater bodily control, finer coordination of hands, eyes, and feet, more strength, and the utilization of some of the basic skills acquired in previous grades.

It has been found that children in the intermediate grades and sometimes as low as third grade can engage satisfactorily in various types of team games such as basketball, soccer, softball, flag football, and volleyball. These games as played at the high school or college level are ordinarily too highly organized and complex for the majority of intermediate level children. It is therefore necessary to modify these activities to meet the needs and interests of this age level. By way of illustration let us consider the game of basketball as played at the high school or college level.

Players at these levels use the regulation size basketball of 29½ inches in circumference and the goal is at a height of 10 feet. For children at the intermediate level the game could be modified by using a smaller ball and lowering the goal. At this level more simple strategies also would be used in playing the game. Teachers should use their own ingenuity along with the help of children in modifying the highly organized games to adjust them for suitability for specific groups of intermediate level children.

One approach to the introduction of the more highly organized team games is the use of *preparatory* games. These contain many of the same skills used in the advanced games. These games are within the capacity of children at this age level and provide them with an opportunity to learn many of the basic skills and some of the rules of the more advanced games.

Rhythmic Activities

Those human movement experiences that *require* some sort rhythmical accompaniment may be placed in the broad category of rhythmic activities. As in the case of other terms described throughout this book, this description of rhythmic activities is arbitrary and used for purposes of discussion here. I am aware that some authorities consider the meaning of the term *dance* to be broader than the term rhythmic activities. However, the point of view here is that there are certain human experiences that require some form of rhythmical accompaniment that do not necessarily have the same objectives as those ordinarily associated with dance. Moreover, according to my surveys, about 80 percent of the books on elementary school physical education use the term rhythmic activities while the remaining 20 percent use the term dance. It is more likely that dance is a more popular term at the secondary school and college levels.

One approach to the classification of rhythmic activities centers around the kinds of rhythmic experiences that one might wish for elementary school children to have. It is recommended here that these experiences consist of (1) unstructured experiences, (2) semistructured experiences, and (3) structured experiences. It should be understood that in this particular way of grouping rhythmic activities a certain amount of overlapping will occur as far as the degree of structuring is concerned. Although an experience is classified as an unstructured one, there could be some small degree of structuring in certain kinds of situations. With this idea in mind the following descriptions of these three types of elementary school rhythmic activities are submitted.

Unstructured experiences include those in which there is an original or creative response and in which there has been little, if any, previous explanation or discussion in the form of specific directions. The *semi-structured* experiences include those in which certain movements or interpretations are suggested by the teacher, a child, or a group of children. *Structured* experiences involve the more difficult rhythmic patterns associated with the various types of dances. A well-balanced program of elementary school rhythmic activities designed to provide such experiences for children gives consideration to (1) fundamental rhythms, (2) creative rhythms, (3) movement songs (sometimes referred to as singing games), and (4) dances.

At the primary level *fundamental rhythmic activities* found in the loco-motor movements of walking, running, jumping, hopping, leaping, skipping, galloping, and sliding, and the nonlocomotor or axial movements such as twisting, turning, and stretching form the basis for all types of rhythmic patterns. Once the children have developed skill in the fundamental rhythms, they are ready to engage in some of the more complex dance patterns. For example, the comination of walking and hopping to musical accompaniment is the basic movement in the dance known as the *schottische.*

Children at the primary level should be given numerous opportunities to engage in *creative rhythms.* This kind of rhythmic activity helps them to express themselves in just the way the accompaniment "makes them feel" and gives vent to expression so necessary in the life of the child.

The *movement song* is a rhythmic activity suitable for primary age children. In this type of activity children can sing their own accompaniment for the various activity patterns that they use in performing the movement song.

Various kinds of *dances* may be included as a part of the program of rhythmic activities for the primary level. Ordinarily these have simple movement patterns which the child learns before progressing to some of the more complex patterns.

At the intermediate level children can engage in rhythmic activities that are more advanced than those at the primary level. Creative rhythms should be continued and children should have the opportunity to create more advanced movement patterns.

Dance patterns involved in the various kinds of folk dances may be somewhat more complex, provided children have had a thorough background in fundamental rhythms and less complicated folk dances at the primary level. Primary level dances can be individual activities and many of them require dancing with a partner. At the intermediate level, "couple dances" that require closer coordination of movement by partners may be introduced.

Self-Testing Activities

The so-called self-testing activities involve competing against one's self and natural forces. These activities are based upon the child's desire to test his ability in such a way that he attempts to better his own performance. This is a broad term and involves such activities as stunts and tumbling, exercises with or without apparatus, and individual skill proficiency such as throwing for accuracy and/or distance, and jumping for height and distance. Some individuals have resurrected the term *educational gymnastics* to describe these kinds of activities. This term was used around the beginning of this century and was in contrast to the term *medical gymnastics,* which was used to identify activities used to correct certain functional or organic disability or deformity. For our purposes here the term self-testing activities seems more appropriate to describe this broad category. Moreover, in modern times about 80 percent of the elementary school physical education textbooks use the term self-testing activities while only about 20 percent use the term educational gymnastics.

At the primary level, children should be given the opportunity to participate in self-testing activities that are commensurate with their ability. For example, stunts that involve imitations of animals are of great interest to boys and girls at this age level. Tumbling activities that involve some of the simple rolls are also suitable. Simple apparatus activities involving the use of such equipment as horizontal ladders, low parallel bars, low horizontal bars, and climbing ropes can be utilized.

Self-testing activities at the intermediate level should be somewhat more advanced provided the children have had previous experience and teaching in this type of activity at the primary level. Tumbling activities that involve more advanced rolls and various kinds of body springs may be successfully introduced. Children at the intermediate level may continue to take part in apparatus activities using much the same equipment that was used at the primary level but moving to more advanced skills. When properly taught, apparatus activity is greatly enjoyed and is excellent for muscular development, especially for the torso and arms. Certain basic game skills are sometimes considered self-testing activities and pave the way for competence in a variety of sports. These include throwing for distance and accuracy, soccer kicking and dribbling, and throwing and catching various types of balls.

THE TEACHING–LEARNING SITUATION IN ELEMENTARY SCHOOL PHYSICAL EDUCATION

There are certain fundamental phases involved in almost every physical education teaching-learning situation. There are (1) auditory input, (2) visual input, (3) participation, and (4) evaluation. Although these four phases are likely to be weighted in various degrees, they will occur in the teaching of practically every physical education lesson regardless of the type of activity that is being taught. While the application of the various phases may be of a general nature, they nevertheless should be utilized in such a way that they become specific in a particular situation. Depending upon the type of activity being taught—game, rhythmic activity or self-testing activity—the use and application of the various phases should be characterized by flexibility and awareness of the objectives of the lesson.

Auditory-Input Phase

The term *auditory* may be described as stimulation occurring through the sense organs of hearing. In education, the term *input* is concerned with the use of as many media as are deemed necessary for a particular teaching-learning situation. The term *output* is concerned with behaviors or reactions of the learner resulting from various forms of input. Auditory input involves the various learning media that are directed to the auditory sense. This should not be interpreted to mean that the auditory-input phase of the teaching-learning situation is a one-way process. Although much of such input may originate with the teacher, consideration should also be given to the verbal interaction among children and between the children and the teacher.

Physical education provides a most desirable opportunity for learning through direct, purposeful experience. In other words, the physical education learning situation is "learning by doing," or learning through pleasurable physical activity. Although verbalization might well be kept to a minimum, a certain amount of auditory input, which should provide for auditory-motor association, appears to be essential for a satisfactory teaching-learning situation. The quality of "kinesthetic feel" may be described as the process of changing ideas into muscular action and is of primary importance in the proper acquisition of physical education motor skills. It might be said that the auditory-input phase of teaching helps to set the stage for a kinesthetic concept of the particular activity being taught.

Listening experiences are, no doubt, among the most abstract of the learning media used with children. As such, this type of learning experience has been much maligned by some educators. However, it should be pointed out that the child first learns to act on the basis of verbal instructions by others. In this regard it has been suggested that later he learns to guide and direct his own behavior on the basis of his language activities; he literally talks to himself and gives himself instructions.

This point of view is supported by research, which has postulated that speech as a form of communication between children and adults later becomes a means of organizing the child's own behavior. The function that was previously divided between two people—child and adult—later becomes an internal function of human behavior.

Great care should be taken with the auditory-input phase in the physical education teaching-learning situation. The ensuing discussions are intended to suggest to the reader ways in which the greatest benefits can accrue when using this particular learning medium.

Preparing the Children for Listening

Since it is likely that the initial part of the auditory-input phase will originate with the teacher, care should be taken to prepare the children for listening. The teacher may set the scene for listening by relating the activity to the interests of the children. In addition, the teacher should be on the alert to help children develop their own purposes for listening.

In preparing children to listen, the teacher should be aware that it is of importance that the comfort of the children be taken into consideration and that attempts should be made for removing any possible attention-distracting factors. Although evidence concerning the effect of environmental distractions on listening effectiveness is not in great abundance, there is reason to believe that distraction does interfere with listening comprehension. Moreover, it was reported years ago that being able to see as well as hear the speaker is an important factor in listening distraction.

These factors have a variety of implications for the auditory-input phase of the physical education teaching-learning situation. For example, consideration should be given to the placement of children when a physical education activity requires auditory input by the teacher. This means, for instance, that if the teacher is providing auditory input from a circle formation, the teacher should take a position as part of the circle instead of speaking from the center of the circle. Also, it might be well for the teacher to consider that an object, such as a ball, can become an attention-distracting factor when an activity is being discussed. The attention of children is sometimes focused on the ball, and they may not listen to what is being said. The teacher might wish to conceal such an object until time for its use is most appropriate. With reference to the importance of the listener being able to see the speaker, teachers might exercise caution in the use of recordings for rhythmic activities that include instructions on the recording. Particularly with primary level children it might be well for the teacher to use the instructions only for himself or herself and only the musical accompaniment for the children.

Teacher-Child and Child-Child Interaction

It was mentioned previously that the auditory-input phase is a two-way process. As such, it is important to take into account certain factors involving verbal interaction of children with children and teacher with children.

By "democracy" some people seem to mean everyone doing or saying whatever happens to cross his mind at the moment. This raises the question of control, and it should be emphasized that group discussions, if they are to be democratic, must be in control. This is to say that if a group discussion is to succeed it must be under control, and let me stress that democracy implies discipline and control.

Group discussion is a kind of sociointellectual exercise (involving numerous bodily movements, of course) just as basketball is a kind of sociointellectual exercise (involving, too, higher mental functioning. Both imply individual discipline to keep play moving within bounds, and both require moderators (or officials) overseeing, though not participating in, the play in a manner that is objective and aloof from the heat of competition. In brief, disciplined, controlled group discussion can be a training ground for living in a society in which both individual and group interests are profoundly respected—just as games can serve a comparable function.

Another important function in teacher-child verbal interaction is with the time given to questions after the teacher has provided auditory input. The teacher should give time for questions from the group, but should be very skillful in the use of questions. It must be determined immediately whether or not a question is a legitimate one. This implies that the type of questions asked can help to serve as criteria for the teacher to evaluate the auditory-input phase of teaching. For example, if numerous questions are asked, it is apparent that either the auditory input from the teacher was unsatisfactory or the children were not paying attention.

Directionality of Sound

In summarizing recent findings concerned with the directionality of sound, a number of interesting factors can be pointed up. Individuals tend to initiate movements toward the direction from which the sound cue emanates. For example, if a cue is given that instructs the individual to move a body segment or segments to the left, but the verbal cue emanates from the right side of the individual, the initial motor response is to the right, followed by a reverse response to the left. Emphasizing the importance of this it is recommended that when working on direction of motor responses with young children, one should make certain that sound cues come from the direction in which the motor response is made. The point is that children have enough difficulty in discriminating left from right without confusing them further.

Visual-Input Phase

The term *visual* is concerned with images that are obtained through the eyes. Thus, visual input involves the various learning media that are directed to the visual sense.

Various estimates indicate that the visual sense brings us upwards of three-fourths of our knowledge. If this postulation can be used as a valid criterion, the merits of the visual-input phase in teaching physical education are readily discernible. In many cases, visual input, which should provide for visual-motor association, serves as a happy medium between verbal symbols and direct participation in helping teachers further to prepare children for the kinesthetic feel mentioned previously.

In general, there are two types of visual input which can be used satisfactorily in teaching physical education. These are visual symbols and human demonstration (live performance).

Visual Symbols

Included among the visual symbols used in physical education are motion pictures and various kinds of flat or still pictures. One of the disadvantages of the latter centers around the difficulty in portraying movement with a still figure. Although movement is obtained with a motion picture, it is not depicted in third dimension, which causes some degree of ineffectiveness when this medium is used. One valuable use of visual symbols is that of employing diagrams to show the dimensions of activity areas. This procedure may be useful when the teacher is discussing an activity in the room before going on to the outdoor activity area. Court dimensions and the like can be diagramed on a chalkboard, providing a good opportunity for the integration with other areas such as mathematics and drawing to scale.

Human Demonstration

Some of the guides to action in the use of human demonstration follow.

1. If the teacher plans to demonstrate, this should be included in the preparation of the lesson by practicing and rehearsing the demonstration.
2. The teacher does not need to do all the demonstrating; in fact, in many cases it may be much more effective to have one or more children demonstrate. Since the teacher is expected to be a skilled performer, a demonstration by a child will oftentimes serve to show other children that one of their peers can perform the activity and that they should be able to do it also.
3. A demonstration should be based on the skill and ability of a given group of children. If it appears to be too difficult for them, they might not want to attempt the activity.
4. When at all possible, a demonstration should parallel the timing and conditions of when it will be put into practice. However, if the situation is one in which the movements are complex or done with

great speed, it might be well to have the demonstration conducted on a slower basis than that involved in the actual performance situation.

5. The group should be arranged so that everyone is in a favorable position to see the demonstration. Moreover, the children should be able to view the demonstration from a position where it takes place. For example, if the activity is to be performed in a lateral plane, children should be placed so that they can see it from this position.

6. Although auditory input and human demonstration can be satisfactorily combined in many situations, care should be taken that auditory input is not lost, because the visual sense offsets the auditory sense; that is, one should not become an attention-distracting factor for the other. It will be up up to the teacher to determine the amount of verbalization that should accompany the demonstration.

7. After the demonstration has been presented it may be a good practice to demonstrate again and have the children go through the movements with the demonstrator. This provides for the use of the kinesthetic sense together with the visual sense that makes for close integration of these two sensory stimuli.

Participation Phase

Direct, purposeful experience is the foundation of all education. Because physical education activities are motor in character, there is a near-ideal situation for learning in this particular area of the elementary school curriculum. The child needs to get his hands on the ball, feel his body coordinated in the performance of a stunt, or dance the folkdance in order to gain a full appreciation of the activity. There is an opportunity in a well-taught physical education lesson for learning to become a part of the child's physical reality, providing for a pleasurable concrete experience, rather than an abstract one. For this reason the following considerations should be kept in mind in connection with the participation phase of teaching.

1. The class period should be planned so that the greatest possible amount of time is given to participation.
2. If the activity does not progress as expected in the participation

phase, perhaps the fault may lie in the procedures used in the auditory- and visual-input phases. Participation then becomes a criterion for the evaluation of former phases.

3. The teacher should take into account the fact that the original attempts in learning an activity should meet with a reasonable degree of success.
4. The teacher should constantly be aware of the possibility of fatigue of children during participation and should understand that individual differences in children create a variation with regard to how rapidly fatigue takes place.
5. Participation should be worthwhile for every child, and all children should have the opportunity to achieve. Procedures that call for elimination of participants should be avoided lest some individuals do not receive the full value from participation.
6. The teacher should be ever on the alert to guide and direct learning, thus making the physical education period a teaching learning period.
7. During the participation phase, the teacher should constantly analyze performance of children in order to determine those who need improvement in skills. Behaviorisms of children should be observed while they are engaging in physical education activities. For example, various types of emotional behavior might be noted in game situations that might not be indicated in any other school activity.
8. Problems involved during participation should be kept in mind for subsequent evaluation of the lesson with the children.

Evaluation Phase

Evaluation is a very important phase of the physical education teaching-learning situation, and, yet, perhaps one of the most neglected aspects of it. For instance, it is not an uncommon procedure to have the physical education class period end at the signal of the bell, with the children hurrying and scurrying from the activity area without an evaluation of the results of the lesson.

Children should be given the opportunity to discuss the lesson and to suggest ways in which improvement might be effected. When this procedure is followed, children are placed in a problem-solving situation and desirable learning is more likely, with the teacher guiding learning rather than dominating the situation in a direction-giving type of procedure. Also, more and better continuity is likely to be provided from one lesson to another when time is taken for evaluation. In addition, children are much more likely to develop a clearer understanding of the purposes of physical education if they are given an opportunity to discuss the procedures involved in the lesson.

Ordinarily, the evaluation phase should take place at the end of the lesson. Experience has shown that a satisfactory evaluation procedure can be effected in three to six minutes, depending upon the nature of the activity and upon what actually occurred during a given lesson. Under certain circumstances, if an activity is not proceeding well in the participation phase, it may be desirable to stop the activity and carry out what is known as a "spot" evaluation. This does not mean that the teacher should stop an activity every time the situation is not developing according to plan. A suggestion or hint to children who are having difficulty with performance can perhaps preclude the need for having all of the children cease participation. On the other hand, if the situation is such that the needs of the group will best be met by a discussion concerning the solution of a problem, the teacher is indeed justified in stopping the activity and conducting an evaluation "on the spot."

Teachers should guard against stereotyping the evaluation phase of the physical education lesson. This implies that the teacher should look for developments during the participation phase of the lesson that might well serve as criteria for evaluation at the end of the lesson. If the evaluation phase is always started with the question, "Did you like it?", this part of the lesson will soon become meaningless and merely time consuming for the children. Depending upon what actually occurred during the participation phase of the lesson, the following general questions might be considered by the teacher when beginning the evaluation phase with the children.

1. Should we review briefly what we learned today?
2. What are some of the things we learned today?
3. What do we have to do or know in order to be a good performer in this game?
4. What did today's activity do for our bodies? Did it help us to have better control over our feet and legs? Did it improve our ability to throw? Did you find that you had to breathe much faster when you played this game?

5. What were some of the things you liked about the game we played today?
6. Can you think of any ways that we might improve the dance we learned today?

Questions such as these place children in a problem-solving situation and consequently provide for a more satisfactory learning situation. Moreover, this procedure is likely to provide a better setting for a child-centered physical education lesson, because children have an opportunity to discuss together ways and means for improvement in the performing of activities.

A very important feature of the evaluation phase is that the teacher has an opportunity to evaluate teaching procedures with a given group of children. In other words, the teacher should have a better understanding of how well the lesson was taught when able to hear firsthand the expressions of the children who participated.

PLANNING PHYSICAL EDUCATION LESSONS

The term *lesson plan* is the name given to a statement of achievements, together with the means by which these are to be attained as a result of the physical education activities participated in during a specified amount of time that a group spends with the teacher.

The success of any elementary school physical education program will depend to a large extent upon the daily physical education experiences of children. This implies that lessons in physical education should be carefully planned the same as in other curriculum areas.

Physical education lesson planning should take into account those factors that indirectly and directly influence the teaching-learning situation. This means that the teacher must consider class organization as a very important factor when daily lessons are planned, because various considerations associated with it can have an indirect influence on the physical education learning situation. For example, it will be desirable for the teacher to effect a plan of class organization that (1) is conducive to carrying out the objectives of the lesson, (2) provides sufficient activity for each child, and (3) provides for efficient and optimum use of facilities and equipment. After sufficient consideration has been given to ways and means of class organization in developing the physical education lesson, the teacher should also take into account the essential characteristic features that directly influence the teaching-learning situation. In this regard, it is strongly emphasized that teachers might well devise their own lesson outlines and patterns. This procedure appears to be essential if teachers are to profit by the flexibility that is inherent in a plan that fits their own needs. With this idea in mind, the following lesson plan outline, indicating some of the features that might be incorporated into a physical education plan, is submitted as a guide for the reader.

1. *Objectives:* A statement of goals that the teacher would like to see realized during the lesson.
2. *Content:* A statement of the physical education learning activities in which the class will engage during the lesson.
3. *Class Procedures:* A brief commentary of procedures to be followed in conducting the lesson, such as (1) techniques for initiating interest and relating previous teaching-learning situations to the present lesson, (2) auditory input, (3) visual input, (4) participation, and (5) evaluation.
4. *Teaching Materials:* A statement of essential materials needed for the lesson.

If the teacher is to provide physical education learning experiences that contribute satisfactorily to total development of children, there must be a clear perspective of the total learning that is expected from the area of physical education. This implies that in order to provide for progression in physical education activities there must be some means of preserving continuity from one class period to another. Consequently, each individual lesson becomes a link in a chain of physical education learnings that contributes to the total development of the child. Experience has shown that the implementation of this theory into reality can be most successfully accomplished by wise and careful lesson planning.

INTEGRATION OR SEGREGATION OF BOYS AND GIRLS FOR ACTIVITIES

In the early history of physical education in the United States the integration of boys and girls for physical education was frowned upon at any grade level. In the 1920s many public elementary school playgrounds segregated boys and girls by having *girls'* and *boys'* days scheduled for use of playground apparatus. In some instances boys and girls could participate at the same time, but activity areas were restricted for use by each of the sexes.

As physical education became more widespread as a curriculum offering in elementary schools it became more or less a common practice to have boys and girls participate together. This may have been done as a matter of convenience because of the lack of departmentalization of classes in the elementary school along with insufficiency of facilities to accommodate separate units for the sexes.

Over the years there have been numerous pronouncements made with reference to when and if elementary school boys and girls should be segregated for participation in physical education activities. In modern times such factors as changes in female behavior along with greater assertiveness of the female personality have caused educators and others to view this phenomenon in a somewhat different light.

As far as elementary school-age children are concerned, the general recommendation over a long period of years suggested that boys and girls be segregated for certain activities, particularly those involving strength factors and physical skill levels. The validity of this recommendation has remained questionable, because as previously mentioned there are certain factors in elementary school organization that militate against segregation of boys and girls.

In the final analysis, it will remain the responsibility of each individual teacher to see that all children—boys and girls alike—are afforded an opportunity for their physical, social, emotional, and intellectual needs to be met through the physical education experience. Essentially, this implies grouping children in some way by ability regardless of sex. This is to say that some girls will be more highly skilled than some boys at the various grade levels, although on average this may not be the case. For example, some studies have shown that boys are superior to girls in catching performance. In addition, it has been shown that sex differences in the early throwing behavior of children tend to favor boys. At all age levels boys are generally superior to girls in throwing for distance. There is not such a pronounced sex difference in throwing for accuracy, although the performance of boys in this aspect tends to exceed that of girls. Some studies have indicated that as low as kindergarten level boys execute the overarm throw with significantly greater velocity than girls.

The recommendation here is that teachers be guided by their general knowledge of the traits and characteristics of elementary school children and above all to be able to recognize the *individual differences* of children within a given group. When these differences are taken into account it is likely that the best interests of all children will prevail in terms of their physical education experiences.

Chapter 3

THE NATURE OF INTEGRATION IN PHYSICAL EDUCATION

In simplest terms integration means the process of making whole. To integrate is to make whole or to bring together the parts of the whole in functional unity, or to become complete. Notwithstanding the fact that the term *integration* is one that should be reasonably easy to define, there has nevertheless been a certain amount of confusion surrounding the term. That is not an uncommon situation with educational terms that have widespread usage. The more frequently an educational term is used, the greater the possibility that its specific meaning may be lost or distorted.

The interpretation of the term *integration* in its usage throughout this volume is based on the value connotation of wholeness, completeness, and unity inherent in the term. Consequently, there will be singularity of meaning of the term with regard to integration of physical education in the elementary school curriculum through teaching units or through specific subject fields.

SOME ASPECTS OF INTEGRATION IN EDUCATION

Educators appear to use the concept of integration psychologically, sociologically, and pedagogically.

Psychologically, integration is a term which concerns the total personality of the learner. This is to say that the individual is a total being and that all of the elements of the total development of the learner (physical, social, emotional, and intellectual) are highly interrelated and dependent one upon the other.

From the sociological point of view, integration can have a threefold meaning. First, there must be considered the relationship between personalities, such as child with child and child with teacher. Second, there needs to be a desirable relationship between the individual and various agencies of society. And finally, there should be a recognition of the relationships between the various institutions of society.

Pedagogically, integration involves teaching methods and techniques which relate various subject-matter areas and skills through units of learning and specific subject fields for the purpose of providing for problem solving as a way of learning. In other words, it is recognized that all areas of the curriculum in the elementary school in one way or another complement one another in the solution of problems for the individual learner.

It is this aspect of integration (the pedagogical) with which the remainder of this book is fundamentally concerned. It will be the primary purpose throughout this volume to show how physical education may be utilized in such a way as to complement the other curriculum areas and how it can be successfully integrated in the elementary school curriculum. The psychological and sociological aspects of integration will be treated in terms of their relation to the successful application of the pedagogical aspect.

THE FUNCTION OF PHYSICAL EDUCATION IN INTEGRATION

Ideally, physical education contributes to the total growth and development of children. It is for this reason that physical education should be included in the elementary school program on an organized basis as an integral part of the elementary school curriculum. The contribution that physical education makes to the well-rounded growth and development of children should be the primary criterion against which a physical education activity is evaluated before it is included in a child's school experience.

That physical education has an extremely important function in the various aspects of integration should be a foregone conclusion. Nevertheless, the fact remains that some persons who may be placed in the category of general educators have sometimes failed to see the true value of physical education as a medium through which many of the physical, social, emotional, and intellectual needs of children can be met. Consequently, in many cases when physical education is included in the elementary school program, it is considered as something apart from the regular curriculum. In reality, the potentialities of physical education with respect to the worthwhile contribution it can make to the total development of the child should serve as evidence that its inclusion in elementary education is essential. Moreover, physical education has a distinct and direct relationship to the educational concept of integration with respect to its psychological, sociological, and pedagogical implications.

The Psychological Aspect

It has been expressed previously that the psychological aspect of integration concerns the total personality of the learner. This implies essentially that what affects the mind also affects the body. There are numerous metaphysical theories regarding bodily and mental functions. What ever opposition these various theories may have to each other, all of them are fundamentally based on the belief that there is a "oneness" of mind and body. This being the case, the psychological aspect of integration has a distinct bearing on physical education.

Physical education is essentially concerned with learning through physical activity. In that most of our contemporary scientists, educators, and philosophers accept the principle of mind-body relationships, or what might be referred to as psychomotor unity, it would seem that the prevailing practice would be the implementation of this principle. The fact that this is not true is evidenced by referrals to some sports participants as having "all brawn and no brain," or reference to physical education as the "muscle factory." Physical educators cannot be exonerated from all of the blame. Some physical educators themselves, while possibly accepting the mind-body relationship idea in principle, have not always carried it into practice.

At the other extreme, in a few isolated cases some physical educators have placed emphasis on the nonphysical aspect of physical education to the extent that there has been gross neglect of the physical aspect. Either of these extremes can detract from total growth and development to the point where disintegration is likely to take place in a situation that is "environmentally ripe" for building integrated personalities.

Persons who operate elementary school physical education programs at either of these extremes are in reality "taking the child apart" in disintegrating fashion, thus reducing him to a mechanistic state of a pawn to be manipulated by the dead hand of tradition.

Fortunately, the extremes mentioned here do not typify the majority of elementary school physical educations programs. However, strong emphasis is given to the point here lest the beginning teacher or even the experienced teacher fall into the lethargy of inadequate elementary school physical education program planning—planning which should be based on the needs of the child's entire organism.

The Sociological Aspect

It has been stated before that, sociologically, integration is involved in three different ways. These ways consist of relations between personalities, relations between individuals and various agencies of society, and relations between the various institutions of society. The primary concern here will be with the sociological aspect of integration which pertains to the relations between personalities.

There are a number of valid reasons why physical education functions desirably in this aspect of integration. Essentially the human being is a social being. Physical education has an excellent opportunity to capitalize upon this factor, because the very nature of most physical education activities is such that some sort of positive or negative reaction between individuals is almost unavoidable. For example, team or group activities obligate the individual to operate as a cooperative member for the success of the group. In this situation it is necessary to sacrifice self-gain for the benefit of the group. Thus, physical education activities of a group nature involve the fundamental principles of democracy. In this general regard it is interesting to note that holding hands in a circle game has important connotations for social interaction through *tactile communication*. Some writers have called attention to the possibilities of this by suggesting that better human relations can be obtained through intrinsic tactile communication in the utilization of activities requiring *touch.* In fact, some studies have shown that such tactile communication provides a basis for the attraction that is necessary for black and white children to form positive relationships. More specifically, it has been demonstrated that recorded incidents of tactile interaction between black children and white children were equivalent to those between white children and white children.

For a further understanding of the implications of physical education in the sociological aspect of integration, it might be well to consider some of the social needs of children. In this connection, there appears to be a certain amount of overlapping with regard to just how the various needs should be categorized. Nevertheless, a survey of the literature on children's needs reveals that many authorities agree that basically there are at least two important social needs that should be met. These include the need for belonging (involving acceptance and approval of the group) and the need for affection (involving acceptance and approval of persons).

The well-planned elementary school physical education program, if it is to contribute to the total growth and development of the child, must help to meet these basic social needs. How, then, can these needs be met through physical education? What can physical education do to make the child feel wanted or to fulfill the need for belonging? Certainly the program must be planned in such a way that all children can take part so that there are no "fringers" or "isolates" who do not get into the activity. When all children have an opportunity to participate in activities suited to their needs and abilities, an ideal situation is developed for meeting the need for belonging and being an accepted member of the group.

The need for affection is closely related to the need for belonging. With relatively few exceptions, children want to be accepted members of the group, and at the same time they are in great need for love and affection. In physical education activities the need for affection may be at least partly met through various means of praise and encouragement when a child is performing a skill to the maximum limits of his capacity. Comments such as "Good try, Mary!" "Nice going, Bobby!" and "You can do it, George!" prevail in elementary school physical education classes where good child-child and teacher-child relations exist. This kind of atmosphere helps the child to feel that his teacher and classmates have an interest in him.

Thus elementary school physical education provides a most desirable laboratory setting for human relations. In the well-planned program a high level of socialization can be achieved, and this achievement is essential in the sociological aspect of integration.

The Pedagogical Aspect

The pedagogical aspect of integration can take place in at least two different ways. First, it may be concerned with procedures in teaching which bring together various subject matter areas through units of work, with these subjects making contributions to the development of the concepts and understandings of the unit. Second, pedagogical integration may involve the relation between two or more subject-matter fields in such a way that the content of each area helps to provide for a better realization of the understandings to be developed in the other. In many elementary school programs both of these approaches are practiced, but in most cases only the so-called traditional subject-matter areas are involved. In many cases physical education has not been considered a legitimate member of the curriculum family. From its introduction into the elementary school program of activities, physical education has been thought of as a special subject, and as such has experienced difficulty in gaining its rightful place as an indispensable partner alongside other curriculum areas. This is indeed an unfortunate situation, because there are numerous physical education experiences which complement other subject areas and enrich other learning activities for children.

For some time now a great deal of emphasis has been placed on the idea that each experience of the child involves his entire organism. Moreover, general opinion indicates that it is impossible to set aside certain experiences as being entirely and exclusively physical, social, emotional, or intellectual. In that each and every experience of the child brings about some sort of change in his entire organism, it seems logical to assume that educational efforts should not be limited to isolated learnings of a single subject-matter area.

It should be understood that learning can take place well through problem solving and that problem solving is a way of human learning. It should be further understood that solution of problems requires subject matter from various fields. The fact that physical education can make such an outstanding contribution to total growth and development indicates that its possibilities for integration should be thoroughly explored.

ADVANTAGES IF INTEGRATING PHYSICAL EDUCATION IN THE CURRICULUM

There are various reasons why it is advantageous to integrate physical education with the other curriculum areas. Some of these advantages may be stated as follows.

Provision is made for a greater variety of activities in units of work. When physical education is integrated within units of work, more learning activities are available in which children may participate. Consequently, children have a better chance to solve the problems of the unit because they have another medium for problem solving. For example, if a class is studying a unit on "Life in Colonial America," a committee may be formed to discover what the colonists did for recreation, the types of games in which they participated, and the kinds of dances they enjoyed. This activity enriches the unit and gives the children a better understanding of life in Colonial America.

Provision is made for a wider background for physical education activities.
When all areas of the curriculum are drawn upon in the process of
solving a problem, there is a better opportunity to provide a wider
background for physical education activities. As a consequence there is a
possibility of another avenue of learning in the solving of problems of a
unit, and at the same time physical education is motivated.

Provision is made for greater unity in the school day. When physical
education is integrated with the other curriculum areas, there is a greater
likelihood that teachers as well as the children will consider it a part of
the daily program rather than an activity divorced from the regular
program of school activities.

The problem of time allotment for physical education may be simplified.
Many elementary schools continue to make the transition from an unor-
ganized to an organized program of physical education. This is to say
that the trend continues to include physical education in the elementary
school on an organized basis rather than to provide for play activities
only in a haphazard way through recess and free play.

With an already full program, some school administrators are reluc-
tant to add more subjects to an overcrowded curriculum. When a new
area is introduced into the elementary school curriculum, room must
be made for it in the school day by crowding out another area or by
lengthening the time that children are in school during the day. Another
possibility is to take a small amount of time from each of the established
subject areas. It is more likely that school administrators and teachers
will subscribe to a plan of this nature, especially if the new subject is one
which can be successfully integrated with the established subjects. In that
physical education falls into this category, the problem of time allotment
should be simplified when physical education is introduced in the elementary school program on an organized basis.

TEACHING RESPONSIBILITY

A question to be raised is: Who should assume the responsibility
for the integration of physical education in the elementary school
curriculum—the physical education teacher or the classroom teacher.
The answer is that its success will depend upon the collaboration and
cooperation of both. It must be remembered that the physical education
activities used for integration should be considered as learning activities
in the same way that other learning activities are used in a given curricu-

lum area. Thought of in these terms, then, for the most part, the procedure should be used during the time allotted to the particular curriculum area in question. The function of the physical education teacher could be to furnish the classroom teacher with suitable physical education activities to use in the development of skills and concepts. This is to say that the classroom teacher is familiar with the skills and concepts to be developed, and similarly the physical education teacher should know which activities could be adapted for use to develop the skills and concepts.

Now, this does not necessarily mean that the procedure is always carried out by the classroom teacher, because sometimes it can be appropriate for the physical education teacher to do so. By working together the physical education teacher and the classroom teacher can plan lessons to be taught either during the time allotted to physical education or to the time allotted to the given subject area. The following two simulated teaching-learning situation are intended to illustrate this point. The first situation is one in which the physical education is teaching a dance during the physical education period and relating it to *fractions*. The second situation depicts a classroom teacher teaching a similar lesson with an active game to her own class.

Lesson Taught by the Physical Education Teacher

The name of this rhythmic activity is *Pop Goes the Weasel* and any suitable recording can be used for the accompaniment. Groups of three with hands joined, form a small circle. These groups are arranged in a large circle, as in the following diagram.

Each group walks around counterclockwise until the strain "Pop goes the weasel" is heard on the recording. At this time one child is "popped" under the joined hands of the other two and sent to the next couple in the large circle. Progression of those "popped" is counterclockwise. Before starting the dance, it must be decided which person in each group will be "popped" through, and the sequence in which the other two will be "popped" through.

In this particular instance the physical education teacher has become aware of a difficulty in getting boys and girls to choose partners with each other in some of the activities they have been playing. Because of this he feels that possibly some rhythms and square dancing could help them to overcome this problem. He feels also that it may be necessary to provide a certain amount of motivation for rhythms, particularly for the boys.

TEACHER: Boys and girls, when reading about sports events in the paper the other day, I came across some sentences that I thought would be of interest to you. In a story about a football game, one sentence said, "The halfback danced down the field." In another report it said, "The runner danced back and forth off of first base." As I thought about this, it occurred to me that dancing might be a good way to develop some of the skills needed to play well in sports and games. Have any of you ever heard of how rhythm and dancing could help to make better players?

CHILD: Gee, I never thought of it that way before.

CHILD: Me, either.

TEACHER: Mrs. Mason tells me that you have been working on fractions. Well, we are going to do a dance today that has a great deal to do with fractions. Please form a large circle with a boy and a girl in every other place. (*Children form the circle.*) We are going to learn a dance called "Pop Goes the Weasel." Maybe some of you have heard the tune before. Let me see the hands of those who have. (*Some children indicate that they are familiar with the tune.*) Do you remember the other day in Mrs. Mason's class when you were studying fractions, what she said the bottom number tells us?

CHILD: I think it was how many parts something is divided into.

TEACHER: Yes, that's right, and now we are going to divide our large circle into groups of three. Starting here, we will form small circles with three persons in each small circle with hands joined. (*The teacher demonstrates with the first group of three to his left.*) Now each group is a circle made up of three persons. If something is divided into three parts, what do we call the name of each part?

CHILD: One-third?

TEACHER: Yes, that's right. Can someone tell me how many thirds make a whole?

CHILD: Three?

CHILD: (Aside to another child) Oh! I see now what Mrs. Mason meant the other day.

TEACHER: All right. Now let's have each person in the small circles take the name of either First-Third, Second-Third, or Last-Third. Just take a minute to decide within your own circle who will take each part. (*The teacher demonstrates with one of the small circles.*) Let me see the hands of all the First-Thirds, the Second-Thirds, the Last-Thirds. Now here is something that is very important. The magic word in this dance is "Pop." That is, if the words of the tune were to be sung. We will move to the right in our own circles. When we come to the part of the music where the word "Pop" would be sung, the person in each circle with the name First-Third will pop under the arms of the other two persons in his circle and become a part of the circle to his right. The people in the small circles will immediately begin to walk again, and this time on the word "Pop" the person named Second-Third will leave his circle. The next time the person named Last-Third leaves. Who do you think will pop the next time?

CHILD: Would we all start over again with First-Third?

TEACHER: Yes, that's right and we will continue that way until the record has finished playing. I am going to play a part of the record for you. This time I want you to listen to the music, and when you hear the part where you pop into the next circle raise your hand so that we can make sure that you will know when to pop. Listen for the chord to start.

(*Children participate in the dance, and after the record is played through once the teacher evaluates the activity with them.*)

TEACHER: What were some of the things you noticed that you thought were good about our first attempt at this dance?

CHILD: We all seemed to go in the right direction and didn't get mixed up.

CHILD: We kept time pretty well.

TEACHER: What were some of the things you liked about it?

CHILD: I liked always being in a different circle.

CHILD: Well it made me catch on to fractions better.

CHILD: Me, too. We ought to do arithmetic like that in our class.

TEACHER: You think it was easier to learn fractions that way? Be sure to tell that to Mrs. Mason.

CHILD: I'll say and it was a lot more fun.

TEACHER: What were some of the ways we might improve it if we tried it another time?

CHILD: We ought to try to all pop at the same time.

CHILD: Maybe we shouldn't try to go around the circle so fast.

TEACHER: Yes, those are all good suggestions. Personally, I think it was rather well done for our first attempt.

Lesson Taught By The Classroom Teacher

This procedure illustrates how a better understanding of fractions might be developed by participating in the game *Triple Change*.

All of the players except three form a circle. The remaining three stand in the center of the circle. The players in the circle count off by threes and the players in the center are numbered 1, 2, and 3. The players in the center take turns calling out their own numbers. When one of them calls a number (1, 2, or 3), the players in the circle who have that number attempt to change places. If a player is caught, he changes places with the caller.

TEACHER: Today we are going to play a game called Triple Change. What do you think the word "triple" means? When we think of "triplets," what number do we think of?

CHILD: Three?

TEACHER: Yes, Frank, how did you know that?

CHILD: I saw some triplets on television. There were three people who looked alike.

TEACHER: Now, I would like to have three of you be a set of triplets. (*Three children volunteer.*) All right. Will you three stand here by me. Do you remember another word that we used in arithmetic class yesterday that is related to three?

CHILD: Was it third?

TEACHER: Yes (*pointing to each player in the center of the circle*), first, second, third. Now, beginning at your left, let each third put up his right hand. What part of a whole set of triplets is "one"?

CHILD: One part.

TEACHER: Yes, but what part?

CHILD: Oh! I see, one third.

TEACHER: Yes, that's it, one third. Who can write one third on the board? (*Child writes it on the board.*) (*Teacher writes* ⅓ = 1 *on the board.*) Now let's play the game.

Form a circle. The set of triplets remain here by me. Those of you in the circle count off in groups of three, and remember your number. All right, fine. Now let's have all of the 1s raise their hands, the 2s, the 3s. Very good. Now be sure to remember your number. The triplets 1, 2, and 3 in the center will be "callers" and they will take turns in calling their numbers. When a number is called, all who have that number must quickly change places with each other. You may do this by changing with a neighbor or running through the circle. The center players take turns calling. If the first one does not get a place, then the second one calls. Should the first succeed in catching one, the player caught will wait his turn in the center until number 2 and number 3 have had a turn at calling before he calls a number. Let's try it once for practice. Fred, call your number.

(After the demonstration, the game is played for a time, and then the teacher evaluates with the class.)

TEACHER: What were some of our problems?

CHILD: Some kids did not remember their numbers and ran at the wrong time.

CHILD: Sometimes it was hard to find a place.

CHILD: Some kids didn't run when their number was called.

TEACHER: Well, now, what do you suppose we could do about some of these things?

(After some discussion, the following decisions were made by the group.)

1. The players in the circle should hold hands, letting only the numbers called go.
2. The players who did not move, or moved at the wrong time, would have to pay a forfeit.
3. When caught three times, a player would be eliminated. (The purpose of this was to discourage players from being deliberately caught in order to become a caller.)

COGNITIVE PHYSICAL EDUCATION

The approach that I have found best suited for the integration of physical education in the elementary school curriculum is what I have identified as *cognitive physical education.* Some years ago I introduced to the literature the concept of dividing physical education into three separate but interrelated and interdependent branches. One of these was cognitive physical education. The other two were identified as *curricular physical education* and *compensatory physical education.* Although we are concerned primarily with cognitive physical education, it seems appropriate to explain the meaning and purpose of the other two branches.

Curricular physical education is the basic branch with which most readers will be familiar. It implies that physical education should be a curriculum area in the elementary school curriculum in the same manner as mathematics is a curriculum area, or science is a curriculum area, and so on. Such factors as sufficient facilities, adequate time allotment, and above all, good teaching, should be provided to carry out the most desirable physical education learning experiences for children. A curriculum that is child-oriented and scientifically developed should be provided as would be the case with the language arts curriculum or the social studies curriculum or any other curriculum in the elementary school. It is in this branch that the child should learn to move efficiently and effectively and to learn the various kinds of motor skills. This should include the locomotor skills, auxiliary skills, and skills of propulsion and retrieval needed for satisfactory performance in active games, rhythmic activities, and self-testing activities.

Compensatory physical education attempts to correct various types of child learning disabilities which may stem from an impairment of the central nervous system and/or have their roots in certain social or emotional problems of children. This branch of physical education, most often through the medium of *perceptual-motor development,* involves the correction, or at least some degree of improvement, of certain motor deficiencies, especially those associated with fine coordination. What some specialists have identified as a "perceptual-motor deficit" syndrome is said to exist with certain neurologically handicapped children. An attempt may be made to correct or improve fine motor control problems through a carefully developed sequence of motor competencies which follow a definite hierarchy of development. This may occur through a structured perceptual-motor program which is likely to be dependent upon a series of systematic exercises. Or, it can occur through compensatory physical education which attempts to provide for these corrections or improvement by having children engage in physical education activities where perceptual-motor developmental factors may be inherent. This procedure tends to be much more fun for children and at the same time is more likely to be free from emotionally traumatizing situations sometimes attendant in some structured perceptual-motor programs.

Although compensatory physical education and cognitive physical education are essentially based on the same concept, the manner in which these two approaches are used should not be confused. It could be said that compensatory physical education is essentially concerned with education *of* the physical, while cognitive physical education is concerned with education *through* the physical. (*Note:* For a detailed account of compensatory physical education the reader is referred to: Humphrey, James H., *Improving Learning Ability Through Compensatory Physical Education*, Springfield, Illinois, Charles C Thomas Publisher, 1976.)

THE THEORY OF COGNITIVE PHYSICAL EDUCATION

The physical education learning medium is concerned with how children can develop skills and concepts in other curriculum areas while actively engaged in certain kinds of physical education activities. Although all children differ in one or more characteristics, the fact remains that they are more *alike* than they are different. The one common likeness of all children is that they all *move*. Cognitive physical education is based essentially on the theory that children will learn better when what we could call *academic learning* takes place through pleasurable physical activity. That is, when the *motor* component operates at a maximal level in skill and concept development in school subject areas essentially oriented to *verbal* learning. This is not to say that *motor* and *verbal* learning are two mutually exclusive kinds of learning, although it has been suggested that at the two extremes the dichotomy appears justifiable. It is recognized that in verbal learning, which involves almost complete abstract symbolic manipulations, there may be, among others, such motor components as tension, subvocal speech, and physiological changes in metabolism which operate at a minimal level. It is also recognized that in motor activity where the learning is predominantly motor in nature, verbal learning is evident, although perhaps at a minimal level. For example, in teaching a physical education activity, there is a certain amount of verbalization (talking) in developing a kinesthetic concept of the particular activity that is being taught.

The procedure of learning through physical education involves the selection of an activity such as an active game, rhythmic activity, or self-testing activity which is taught to the children and used as a learning activity for the development of a skill or concept in a specific subject area. An attempt is made to arrange an active learning situation so that a fundamental intellectual skill or concept is practiced or rehearsed in the course of participating in the physical education activity.

Essentially, there are two general types of such activities. One type is useful for developing a specific concept where the learner *acts out* the concept and thus is able to visualize as well as to get the *feel* of the concept. Concepts become a part of the child's physical reality, so to speak, as the child participates in the activity where the concept is inherent. An example of such an activity follows.

The concept to be developed is the science concept *electricity travels along a pathway and needs a complete circuit over which to travel.* A physical education activity in which this concept is inherent is *Straddle Ball Roll.*

The children stand one behind the other in relay files with six to ten children in each file. All are in stride position with feet far enough apart so that a ball can be rolled between the legs of the players. The first person in each file holds a rubber playground ball. At a signal the person in front of each file starts the activity by attempting to roll the ball between the legs of all the players on his team. The team that gets the ball to the last member of its file first in the manner described scores a point. The last player goes to the head of his file, and this procedure is continued with a point scored each time for the team that gets the ball back to the last player first. After every player has had an opportunity to roll the ball back the team that has scored the most points is declared the winner.

In applying this physical education activity to develop the concept the first player at the head of each file becomes the electric switch which opens and shuts the current. The ball is the electric current. As the ball rolls between the children's legs it moves right through if all of the legs are properly lined up. When a leg is not in the proper stride, the path of the ball is impeded and the ball rolls out. The activity has to be stopped until the ball is recovered and the correction made in the position of the leg. The circuit has to be repaired (the child's leg) before the flow of electricity (the roll of the ball) can be resumed.

The second type of physical education activity helps to develop skills by using these skills in highly interesting and stimulating situations. Repetitive practice for the development of skills related to specific concepts can be utilized. An example of this type of physical education activity follows.

This activity is an adaptation of the game *Steal the Bacon* and is used for the practice on *initial consonants.* Children are put into two groups of seven each. The members of both teams are given the letters *b, c, d, h, m, n,* and *p* or any other initial consonants with which they have been having difficulty. The teams face each other about ten feet apart as in the following diagram.

b		p
c		n
d		m
h	beanbag	h
m	(bacon)	d
n		c
p		b

The teacher calls out a word such as *ball,* and the two children having the letter *b* run out to grab the beanbag. If a player gets the beanbag back to his line, he scores two points for his team. If his opponent tags him before he gets back, the other team scores one point. The game ends when each letter has been called. The scores are totalled and the game is repeated with the children being identified with different letters.

FACTORS WHICH FACILITATE CHILD LEARNING THROUGH COGNITIVE PHYSICAL EDUCATION

During the early school years, and at ages six to eight particularly, it is likely that learning is limited frequently by a relatively short attention span rather than only by intellectual capabilities. Moreover, some children who do not appear to think or learn well in abstract terms can more readily grasp concepts when given an opportunity to use them in an applied manner. In view of the fact that the child is a creature of movement, and also that he is likely to deal better in concrete rather than abstract terms, it would seem to follow naturally that the physical education learning medium is well-suited for him.

The above statement should not be interpreted to mean that I am suggesting that learning through movement-oriented experiences (motor learning) and passive learning experiences (verbal learning) are two different kinds of learning. The position is taken here that *learning is learning,* even though in the physical education approach the motor component may be operating at a higher level than in most of the traditional types of learning activities.

The theory of learning accepted here is that learning takes place in terms of reorganization of the systems of perception into a functional and integrated whole because of the result of certain stimuli. This implies that problem solving is a way of desirable and worthwhile human learning and that learning can take place well through problem solving. In a physical education learning situation that is well planned, a great deal of consideration should be given to the inherent possibilities for learning in terms of problem solving. In this approach opportunities abound for near-ideal teaching-learning situations because of the many problems to be solved. Using active games as an example the following sample questions asked by children indicate that there is a great opportunity for reflective thinking, use of judgment and problem solving in this type of experience.

1. Why didn't I get to touch the ball more often?
2. How can we make it a better game?
3. Would two circles be better than one?
4. How can I learn to throw the ball better?

Another very important factor to consider with respect to the physical education learning medium is that a considerable part of the learnings of young children are motor in character, with the child devoting a good proportion of his attention to skills of a locomotor nature. Furthermore, learnings of a motor nature tend to usurp a large amount of the young child's time and energy, and are often closely associated with other learnings. In addition, it is well known by experienced classroom teachers at the primary level that the child's motor mechanism is active to the extent that it is almost an impossibility for him to remain for a very long period of time in a quiet state regardless of the passiveness of the learning situation.

To demand prolonged sedentary states of children is actually, in a sense, in defiance of a basic physiological principle. This is concerned directly with the child's basal metabolism. The term *metabolism* is concerned with physical and chemical changes in the body which involve producing and consuming energy. The rate at which the physical and chemical processes are carried on when the individual is in a state of rest represents his *basal metabolism.* Thus, the basal metabolic rate is indicative of the speed at which body fuel is changed to energy as well as how fast this energy is used.

Basal metabolic rate can be measured in terms of calories per meter of body surface, with a calorie representing a unit measure of heat energy in food. It has been found that, on the average, basal metabolism rises from birth to about two or three years of age, at which time it starts to decline until the ages of 20 to 24. Also, the rate is higher for boys than for girls. With the high metabolic rate, and therefore the greatest amount of energy occurring during the early school years, deep consideration might well be given to learning activities through which this energy can be utilized. Moreover, it has been observed that there is an increased attention span of primary age children during participation in physical education activities. When a task such as a physical education activity is meaningful to a child, he can spend longer periods engaged in it than is likely to be the case in some of the more traditional types of learning activities.

The comments made thus far have alluded to some of the *general* aspects of the value of the physical education learning medium. The ensuing discussions will focus more specifically upon what might arbitrarily be called *inherent facilitative factors* in the physical education learning medium which are highly compatible with child learning. These factors are *motivation, proprioception,* and *reinforcement,* all of which are somewhat interdependent and interrelated.

Motivation

In consideration of motivation as an inherent facilitative factor in learning through physical education, the term could be thought of as it is described in the *Dictionary of Education* — that is, "the practical art of applying incentives and arousing interest for the purpose of causing a pupil to perform in a desired way."

One should also take into account *extrinsic* and *intrinsic* motivation. Extrinsic motivation is described as "the application of incentives that are external to a given activity to make work palatable and to facilitate performance," while intrinsic motivation is the "determination of behavior that is resident within an activity and that sustains it, as with autonomous acts and interests."

Extrinsic motivation has been and continues to be used as a means of spurring individuals to achievement. This most often takes the form of various kinds of reward incentives. The main objection to this type of motivation is that it may tend to focus the learner's attention upon the reward rather than the learning task and the total learning situation.

In general, the child is motivated when he discovers what seems to him to be a suitable reason for engaging in a certain activity. The most valid reason, of course, is that he sees a purpose for the activity and derives enjoyment from it. The child must feel that what he is doing is important and purposeful. When this occurs and the child gets the impression that he is being successful in a group situation, the motivation is intrinsic; it comes about naturally as a result of the child's interest in the activity. It is the premise here that learning through physical education in the form of active games, rhythmic activities, and self-testing contain this *built in* ingredient so necessary to desirable and worthwhile learning.

The ensuing discussions of this section of the chapter will be concerned with three aspects of motivation that are considered to be inherent in the physical education learning medium: (1) motivation in relation to *interest*, (2) motivation in relation to *knowledge of results*, and (3) motivation in relation to *competition*.

Motivation in Relation to Interest

It is important to have an understanding of the meaning of interest as well as an appreciation of how interests function as an adjunct to learning. As far as the meaning of the term is concerned, *interest* could be considered as a state of being, a way of reacting to a certain situation. *Interests* can be thought of as those fields or areas to which a child reacts with interest consistently over an extended period of time.

A good condition for learning is a situation in which a child agrees with and acts upon the learnings that he considers of most value to him. This means that the child accepts as most valuable those things that are of greatest interest to him. To the very large majority of children, physical education experiences are likely to be of the greatest personal value.

Under most circumstances a very high interest level is concomitant with pleasurable physical activities simply because of the expectation of pleasure children tend to associate with such activities. The structure of a learning activity is directly related to the length of time the learning act can be tolerated by the learner without loss of interest. Physical education experiences by their very nature are more likely to be so structured than many of the traditional learning activities.

Motivation in Relation to Knowledge of Results

Knowledge of results is most commonly referred to as *feedback* which is the process of providing the learner with information as to how accurate his reactions were. Or, knowledge of various kinds which the performer received about his performance.

Many learning theorists feel that knowledge of results is the strongest, most important variable controlling performance and learning, and further, that studies have repeatedly shown that there is no improvement without it, progressive improvement with it, and deterioration after its withdrawal. As a matter of fact, there appears to be sufficient objective evidence that indicates that learning is usually more effective when one receives some immediate information on how he is progressing. It would appear rather obvious that such knowledge of results is an important adjunct to learning because one would have little idea of which of his responses was correct. Some learning theorists make the analogy that it would be like trying to learn a task while blindfolded.

The physical education learning medium provides almost instantaneous knowledge of results because the child can actually *see* and *feel* himself throw a ball, or tag or be tagged in a game. He does not become the victim of a poorly constructed paper-and-pencil test, the results of which may have little or no meaning for him.

Motivation in Relation to Competition

Using active games as an example of a physical education activity to discuss the motivational factor of competition we have already described games as *active interaction of children in cooperative and/or competitive situations.* It is possible to have both cooperation and competition functioning at the same time as in the case of team games. While one team is competing against the other, there is cooperation within each group. In this framework it could be said that a child is learning to cooperate while competing. It is also possible to have one group competing against another without cooperation within the group as in the case of games where all children run for a goal line independently and on their own.

The terms *cooperation* and *competition* are antonymous; therefore, the reconciliation of children's competitive needs and cooperative needs is not an easy matter. In a sense, one is confronted with an ambivalent condition, which if not carefully handled could place children in a state of conflict.

Modern society not only rewards one kind of behavior (cooperation), but also its direct opposite (competition). Perhaps more often than not our cultural demands sanction these rewards without provision of clear-cut standards with regard to specific conditions under which these forms of behavior might well be practiced. Thus, the child could be placed in somewhat of a quandary with regard to when to compete and when to cooperate.

Recently it has been found that competition does not necessarily lead to peak performance and may in fact interfere with achievement. In this connection Kohn[1] reported on a survey on the effects of competition on sports, business, and classroom achievement and found that 65 studies showed that cooperation promoted higher achievement than competition, eight showed the reverse and 36 showed no statistically significant difference. It was concluded that the trouble with competition is that it makes one person's success depend upon another's failure, and as a result when success depends on sharing resources, competition can get in the way.

In generalizing on the basis of the available evidence with regard to the subject of competition and children, it seems justifiable to formulate the following concepts.

1. Very young children in general are not very competitive but become more so as they grow older.
2. There is a wide variety in competition among children—that is, some are violently competitive while others are mildly competitive, and still others are not competitive at all.
3. Boys tend to be more competitive than girls.
4. Competition should be adjusted so that there is not a preponderant number of winners over losers.
5. Competition and rivalry produce results in effort and speed of accomplishment.

In physical education teaching-learning situations teachers might well be guided by the above concepts. As far as the competitive aspects of certain physical education activities are concerned, they not only appear

---

[1]Kohn, A., *No Contest: The Case Against Competition*, Boston, Moughton-Mifflin, 1986.

to be a good medium for learning because of the intrinsic motivation inherent in them, but this medium of learning can also provide for competitive needs of children in a pleasurable and enjoyable way.

Proprioception

It was stated earlier that the theory of learning accepted here is that learning takes place in terms of a reorganization of the systems of perception into a functional and integrated whole as a result of certain stimuli. These systems of perception, or sensory processes as they are sometimes referred to, are ordinarily considered to consist of the senses of sight, hearing, touch, smell, and taste. Although this point of view is convenient for some purposes, it greatly oversimplifies the ways by which information can be fed into the human organism. A number of sources of sensory input are overlooked, particularly the senses that enable the body to maintain its correct posture. As a matter of fact, the 60 or 70 pounds of muscle which include over 600 in number that are attached to the skeleton of the averaged-sized man could well be his most important sense organ.

Various estimates indicate that the visual sense brings us more than three fourths of our knowledge. Therefore, it could be said with little reservation that man is *eye-minded.* However, one of my former contemporaries, the late Dr. Arthur Steihaus, a notable physiologist, once reported that a larger portion of the nervous system is devoted to receiving and integrating sensory input originating in the muscles and joint structures than is devoted to the eye and ear combined. In view of this it could be contended that man is also *muscle sense-*minded.

Generally speaking, *proprioception* is concerned with muscle sense. The proprioceptors are sensory nerve terminals that give information concerning movements and position of the body. A proprioceptive feedback mechanism is involved which, in a sense, regulates movement. In view of the fact that children are so movement-oriented, it appears a reasonable speculation that proprioceptive feedback from the receptors of the muscles, skin, and joints may contribute in a facilitative manner when the physical education learning medium is used to develop academic skills and concepts. The combination of the psychological factor of motivation and the physiological factor of proprioception inherent in the physical education learning medium has caused me to coin the term *motor*vation to describe this phenomenon.

One writer once characterized my concept of this in the following manner.

> Humphrey presents highly persuasive evidence for the effectiveness of his concepts. He suggests that sensory experiences arising from muscle action acts as a kind of coordinating process that aids in the integration of visual and auditory input, forming a holistic kind of perceptual experience as a child moves his body and limbs in the activities he has devised.[2]

Reinforcement

In considering the compatibility of physical education learning with reinforcement theory, the meaning of reinforcement needs to be taken into account. An acceptable general description of reinforcement is that there is an increase in the efficiency of a response to a stimulus brought about by the concurrent action of another stimulus. A simple example of this would be when a teacher gives praise and encouragement when a child is engaged in a task. Generally, the same principle applies when athletes refer to the "home court advantage." That is, the home fans are present to spur them on. The basis for contending that physical education activity learning is consistent with general reinforcement theory is that it reinforces attention to the learning task and learning behavior. It keeps the child involved in the learning activity, which is perhaps the major area of application for reinforcement procedures. Moreover, there is perhaps little in the way of human behavior that is not reinforced, or at least reinforcible, by feedback of some sort. The importance of proprioceptive feedback has already been discussed in this particular connection.

In summarizing this discussion, it would appear that physical education activity learning establishes a more effective situation for learning reinforcement for the following reasons.

1. The greater motivation of the children in the physical education learning situation involves emphasis on those behaviors directly pertinent to their learning activities, making these salient for the purpose of reinforcement.
2. The proprioceptive emphasis in physical education activity learn-

---

[2]Cratty, Bryant J., *Physical Expressions of Intelligence*, Englewood Cliffs, New Jersey, Prentice-Hall, 1972, p. 49.

ing involves a greater number of *responses* associated with and conditioned to learning stimuli.

3. The gratifying aspects of physical education activity learning provide a generalized situation of *reinforcers.*

EVIDENCE TO SUPPORT THE THEORY

Any approach to learning should be based, at least to some degree, upon objective evidence produced by experimental research, and this is the subject of the following discussion.

There are a number of acceptable ways of studying how behavioral changes take place in children. In this regard, over a period of years I have conducted numerous controlled studies concerned with the cognitive physical education approach to learning. The findings are suggestive enough to give rise to some interesting conclusions, which may be briefly summarized as follows:

1. In general, children tend to learn certain academic skills and concepts better through the physical education learning medium than through many of the traditional approaches.
2. This approach, while favorable to both boys and girls, appears to be more favorable for boys.
3. This approach appears to be more favorable for children with average and below average intelligence.
4. For children with higher levels of intelligence, it may be possible to introduce more advanced concepts at an earlier age through this approach.

In addition to the above scientific findings, the many successful experiences with the physical education activities recommended throughout this book should encourage teachers and others to use the approach in an effort to help children learn by means of pleasurable and enjoyable experiences.

Cognitive physical education as an approach to the integration of physical education in the elementary school curriculum has come to be designated as the "Humphrey Program of Child Learning Through Motor Activity," and it has received rather widespread recognition.

Statement abstracts about it have been distributed to scholars in 55 countries. The Center for the Study of World Psychologies has distributed some of the research studies about the Program to interested individual and research groups in the Soviet Union and Japan. And, the

Program has been featured in a Voice of American broadcast and distributed to its 35 language centers.

It is difficult to accurately determine the extent of the use of the Humphrey Program for purposes of integration of physical education in the elementary school curriculum. There is reason to believe, however, that various aspects of it are being used in a variety of schools in this country and abroad. Two examples of such use are reported here.

The first is The Saint Martins Church of England Junior Mixed School, Scarborough, Yorkshire. The Headmaster of this school is Mr. F. Smith and the following comment was made in the Church of England Newspaper.

> I recommend these attractive well-illustrated books to teachers of young children and also backward readers. They are designed to help the child to read through physical activities. The format of the readers, together with the frequent language repetition and amusing characters, will encourage the child to explore the reading matters for himself. They will also be useful for reading comprehension because the teacher will be able to observe by the child's actions how well he has understood what he has read. They will stimulate the child's interest in reading and also improve his ability to read.

(This aspect of the Program is concerned with physical education reading content or motor activity stories and involves what I have identified as the AMAV Technique. A detailed account of this technique will be presented in the following chapter.)

The second example of a school using the Program is Windsor Alternative Elementary School in Columbus, Ohio. The following is a statement by Joseph H. Copeland, Principal of the school, and Diane Barnes, Physical Education Teacher.

> Windsor Alternative School of Academic and Physical Excellence is an inner-city school located in the near east side of Columbus. Before 1987, Windsor's profile matched that of many American urban elementary programs: student achievement in mathematics and language arts was below national and local averages, the building's instructional resources, for the most part, were outdated and unusable, and the staff unity and morale had diminished. In the 1987–1988 school year Windsor was restructured as an alternative school.
>
> Together, every member of the new staff and administration developed a mission statement with the belief that children's physical, emotional, social and intellectual growth are interdependent. With this focus the staff began to develop a curriculum which integrated academics and

physical education. At Windsor, the goal was not just the learning of physical education, but increasing learning *through* physical education.

The process, which is used by the Windsor staff to achieve a balance of body and mind through the integrating of academics and physical education, is the formation of policy statements. These policy statements provide the means of creating the interdisciplinary curriculum. There is a bi-weekly physical education integration where an academic objective is brought to the physical education class. Activities used for this purpose are derived from those devised by James H. Humphrey. An example is the ordinal use of numbers and in physical education students can play "Call and Catch" to practice this objective. Reading, mathematics, science, and social study integrations occur in all grade levels during the physical education class throughout the school year.

An interesting feature concerning these two statements is that the first was made in 1965, and the second was made 25 years later in 1990. This suggests something about the longevity of the Program.

Chapter 4

INTEGRATION OF
PHYSICAL EDUCATION AND READING

The areas recommended here for the integration of physical education and reading are: (1) diagnosis through physical education experiences, (2) teaching reading skills and concepts, and (3) physical education reading content.

DIAGNOSIS THROUGH
PHYSICAL EDUCATION EXPERIENCES

A standard general description of the term *diagnosis* is the act of identifying a condition from its signs and symptoms. Applied to reading, diagnosis implies an analysis of reading behavior for purposes of discovering strengths and weaknesses of a child as a basis for more effective guidance of his reading efforts.

Among other things, it is important to try to discover why a child reads as he does, what he is able to read, and what he reads successfully. In addition, we need to know if he is having problems in reading, what these problems are, and the causes of the problems.

In the school situation many diagnostic tests are available for use, and they have various degrees of validity. Studies tend to show that teachers themselves can forecast reading success of first grade children with about as much accuracy as reading readiness tests. It may be that such success in teacher observation has been a part of the reason for what is called *diagnostic teaching* becoming a byword as school systems address their attention to meeting the needs of individual children. Diagnostic teaching simply means that teachers employ observation, recording, and analysis of children's performance in day-to-day reading situations.

Diagnostic Teaching Techniques

Obtaining daily feedback is a key to structuring appropriate day-to-day learning activities, because they are based on the "real" reading performance of the child. It is a better "reading" of where the child is in his skills development. Therefore, in diagnostic teaching, teachers are using such techniques as coding errors made by children while oral reading to prove points in the discussion of material they are reading for a directed reading-thinking activity. In this way the teacher has information about the children's sight vocabulary, word attack application to unfamiliar words in context reading, and comprehension skills.

The every-pupil-response technique is used by the teacher as a diagnostic teaching procedure in many types of situations. With the technique calling for each child in a group to respond to a question or problem by holding up an answer card or signaling with a finger response a choice of answers, the teacher is able to check the performance of all the children. The teacher can observe each child's understanding and interpreting of the material, his application of specific skill to new words as in the case of reading. This technique not only provides information about each child's skills development within a group activity, but it also involves each child consistently throughout the learning and and application of skills. This aspect of maximum involvement of each child within a group activity is particularly inherent in physical education experiences. An example of this is the game *Match Cats* which is described later in the chapter.

It is interesting to note that these diagnostic techniques are geared to observing an individual child's performance within group learning activities. Teachers employing these techniques have reported they are better able to plan further activities for children to meet their individual needs through subgrouping children for additional learning experiences. As a result, the individualizing of instruction, a major objective of schools, becomes a reality.

By using physical education experiences, the use of children's naturally physically-oriented world becomes a positive factor operating to facilitate further interest, as well as more involvement and attending to the learning task. Many children tend to lose their apprehension of an intellectual task when it is "buried" in the context of a physical education experience.

In particular, disabled readers will often perform tasks such as auditory and visual discrimination while engaging in a physical education activity like *Man from Mars, Match Cards,* and *Letter Spot* when they might be saying "I can't do it" in more traditional learning activities. (Descriptions of these activities are presented later in the chapter.) Observations of children with severe reading problems, whose discouragement and frustration initially hamper their willingness even to participate, has found their natural affinity for physical activity has been the starting point of a more accurate assessment of their skill strengths and needs as well as remediation.

The total physical involvement of such children through physical education experiences related to reading appears to act as a means for releasing the emotional blockage that inhibits any attempt to perform the intellectual reading tasks involved. And once these children participate successfully in such activities because of the strengthening of input through the physical education experience, the process of building more positive attitudes toward reading and a feeling that they can learn is begun. Needless to say, once the teacher has observed a higher-level performance of children in this setting, it is important to help the children recognize that they were able, and did, perform the skill involved. Such children need to be shown they *can* and *have* mastered a skill with specific evidence that they have learned.

Four important factors in physical education experiences that the teacher can utilize to determine whether further learning experiences are necessary for skill master are (1) the type of sensory input or modality involved in the reading task inherent in the physical education experience, (2) the accuracy of the child's responses in the reading task, (3) the reaction time of children in performing that reading task, and (4) the self-evaluation of the child of his performance.

Many educators believe that sound instructional programs should be characterized by specific-skill orientation. The impact of establishing behaviorally-stated goals as objectives for instruction can help teachers to move beyond such lesson plan goals as "learning word attack skills" to "being able to identify by name the initial letter of a word given orally" or "being able to give orally another word that begins with the same sound as a word presented visually." In the latter lesson objectives both input and output modality are clearly stated so that a teacher observing such activities can analyze children's performance in regard to sensory modality both for input and output production. Such information helps the teacher to identify those children who consistently give evidence of significant differences in performance when lesson input is basically auditory or visual. Such information helps the teacher to adapt instruction accordingly and thereby assure more meaningful, and more successful, learning-to-read experiences.

Physical education experiences related to reading by their very nature enable the teacher to identify the specific reading skills involved. The reading skills utilized in physical education can be readily identified. An example of this would be the activity *Letter Spot* in which the reading skill is one of visual recognition of upper and lower case letters in order to play the activity. (This activity is explained later in the Chapter.)

The second factor in the physical education experience which a teacher can utilize is the accuracy of children's responses to the reading task inherent in the activity. It can be observed those children who use the specific skill with at least 90 percent accuracy in their responses. This should represent skill mastery at the independent level. Any lower percentage of accuracy would indicate additional experiences are necessary.

The third factor relating to the reaction time of children's performance during the physical education experience helps the teacher to identify the ease and comfort of children in performing a specific task. Reaction time in the present context refers to the amount of time it takes for the onset of a response of a person after receiving a stimulus. By observing the quickness of a child's response to the reading task inherent in the physical education experience the teacher can assess the degree of ease as well as the accuracy of the child's responses. While percentage of accuracy is a useful and necessary tool in determining when a child reaches the point of skill mastery, the ease and comfort of the child during the reading task is also a significant factor. Skill mastery implies operation of an "automatic" level independently.

Of particular concern in consideration of reaction time are those children who have a disability in processing the sensory input with a resulting delay in reaction to the question or task presented. Such impairment can effect auditory, visual, or feeling input. This may be related to the first factor in the use of physical education as a diagnostic tool in which the teacher is observing children's performance in terms of modality used. In the activity *Call and Catch* (described later) the teacher adjusts the timing by momentarily holding the ball before throwing it into the air. In the case of reaction time there may simply be a lesser degree of impairment resulting only in more reaction time necessary to perform the task. The teacher must be aware that children may have this type of disability and attempt to recognize those children who consistently need additional time to respond to the task. It is important to adjust to the needs of such children rather than categorizing their delay in responding as being the result of disinterest or uncooperativeness. Physical education experiences can easily be adapted to such children.

The fourth factor is that of self-evaluation by the children themselves. Children should be encouraged not only to react to the activity itself but also to assess how they did and what they might do to improve their performance of the reading skill involved. It might be a case of looking more carefully at the word, picture, or design cards used in the physical education experience. In such pleasurable activities children appear more willing to examine their performance in the learning tasks involved, and quite realistically as well.

The uniqueness of physical education, therefore, as another means of classroom diagnosis, is that such experiences tend to remove the apprehension of testing procedures and can demonstrate a level of skills development that is possibly more consistent with day-to-day performance. Such performance of the reading skill involved in the physical education experience might even appear higher than when the children are engaged in more traditional reading activities. This higher level performance should then be taken as a more accurate assessment of children's potential level of performance when they are operating under optimum conditions of learning.

Diagnosis of Reading Readiness Skills Through Physical Education

Reading readiness skills are a complex cluster of basic skills including (1) language development in which the child learns to transform *his experience* and *his environment* into language symbols through listening, oral language facility, and a meaningful vocabulary; (2) the skills relating to the mechanics of reading such as left-to-right orientation, auditory and visual discrimination, and recognition of letter names and sounds; and (3) the cognitive processes of comparing, classifying, ordering, interpreting, summarizing, and imagining.

Likewise, sensorimotor skills provide a foundation for these basic skills by sharpening the senses and developing motor skills involving spatial, form, and time concepts. The following list identifies some concepts developed through direct body movement involved in physical education experiences.

1. Body Image
2. Space and Direction
3. Balance
4. Basic Body Movements
5. Eye-Hand Coordination
6. Eye-Foot Coordination
7. Form Perception
8. Rhythm
9. Large Muscle Activity
10. Fine Muscle Activity

These skills are essential to the establishment of a sound foundation for the beginning-to-read experiences of children. Not only can the reading readiness program, structured for the development of these skills, be facilitated through physical education experiences, but diagnosis of progress in skills development can be obtained by teacher observation and children's self-evaluation. Physical education experiences can be utilized effectively to provide meaningful and satisfying learning activities in the reading readiness program. The following physical education experiences are described to indicate the variety of activities that may be employed in the development and assessment of readiness skills.

Language Development

In such activities as the following, concept formation is translated into meaningful vocabulary.

Concept: Classification

Activity: Pet Store

One fairly large Pet Store is marked off at one end of the activity area and a Home at the other end. At the side is a Cage. In the center of the playing area stands the Pet Store Owner. All the children stand in the Pet Store and are given a picture of one kind of pet (for example fish, bird, dog). There should be about two or three pictures of each kind of pet. The Pet Store Owner calls "Fish" (or any of the other pets in the activity). The children who have pictures of fish must try to run from the Pet Store to their new Home without being caught or tagged by the Owner. If they are caught, they must go to the Cage and wait for the next call. The activity continues until all the Pets have tried to get to their new home. Kinds of pets can be changed frequently.

Application: By grouping themselves according to the animal pictures, children are able to practice classifying things that swim, things that fly, and so forth. At the end of the activity the class can count how many fish, dogs, and so forth were caught. All the fish, birds, dogs, and so forth can then form their own line to *swim, fly,* or *walk* back to the Pet Store where new pictures can be given to the children for another game.

Concept: Vocabulary Meaning—Action Words

Activity: What to Play

The children may stand beside their desks. One of the children is selected to be the leader. While that child is coming to the front of the room to lead, the rest of the class begins to sing:

> Mary tell us what to play,
> What to play, what to play,
> Mary tell us what to play,
> Tell us what to play.

(The song is sung to the tune of Mary Had a Little Lamb.)

The leader then says, "Let's play we're fishes," or "Let's wash dishes," or "Let's throw a ball." The leader then performs some action that the other children have to imitate. On a signal the children stop, and a new leader is selected.

Application: This activity gives children an opportunity to act out meanings of words. It helps them to recognize that spoken words represent actions of people as well as things that can be touched.

Concept: Vocabulary Meaning—Left and Right

Activity: Changing Seats

Enough chairs for each child in the group are placed side by side in about four or five rows. The children sit alert, ready to move either way. The teacher calls, "Change right!" and each child moves into the seat to his right. When the teacher calls "Change left!" each child moves left. The child at the end of the row who does not have a seat to move to must run to the other end of the row to sit in the vacant seat there. The teacher can bring excitement to the activity by the quickness of commands or unexpectedness by calling the same direction several times in succession. After each command the first row of children who all find seats may score a point for that row.

Application: This type of activity makes children more aware of the necessity of differentiating left from right. At the beginning of the activity, children may not be able to differentiate directions rapidly. The teacher will need to gear the rapidity of his or her commands according to the skills of the group.

Auditory Discrimination

The following activity shows not only a physical education activity using auditory discrimination skills, but also the way activities can be adapted to other reading skills.

Concept: Auditory Discrimination — Beginning Sounds of Words
Activity: Man from Mars

One child is selected to be the Man from Mars and stands in the center of the activity area. The other children stand behind a designated line at one end of the area. The activity begins when the children call out, "Man from Mars, can we chase him through the stars?" The teacher answers, "Yes, if your name begins like "duck." (Or any other word.) All the children whose name begins with the same beginning sound as *duck* or whatever word is called, chase the Man from Mars until he is caught. The child who tags him becomes the new Man from Mars, and the activity continues.

Application: In order for the children to run at the right time, they must listen carefully and match beginning sounds. If the teacher sees a child not running when he should, individual help can be given. Children can also listen for words beginning like or ending like other words the teacher may use for the key word.

Visual Discrimination

The various activities described here relating to visual discrimination indicate the variety of physical education situations that can be utilized to develop skills or to assess skills development.

Concept: Visual Discrimination
Activity: Match Cats

The teacher makes duplicate sets of cards with pictures or designs on them with as many cards as there are children. The children sit on the surface area. The cards are passed out randomly. On a signal or music playing, the children move around the activity area with specified loco-motor movements such as hopping or skipping. When the music stops or a signal is given, each child finds the person with his duplicate card, joins one hand, and they sit down together. The last couple down becomes the Match Cats for that turn. The children then get up and exchange cards. The activity continues in the same manner with different locomotor movements used.

Application: Depending on the level of skills development of the children, the cards may be pictures of real objects or abstract forms, colors, alphabet letters, and words.

Concept: Visual Discrimination

Activity: Mother May I (An adaption)

The children stand on a line at the back of the activity area. The teacher has cards showing object pairs, similar and different. The teacher holds up one pair of cards. If the paired objects or symbols are the same, the children may take one giant step forward. Any child who moves when he sees an unpaired set of cards must return to the starting line. The object of the activity is to reach the finish line on the opposite side of the playing area.

Application: The teacher may select cards to test any level of visual discrimination. Using pairs of cards for categorizing pictures would utilize concept and language development.

Concept: Visual Discrimination

Activity: Match Cards

Each child in the group is given a different-colored card. Several children are given duplicate cards. There are two chairs placed in the center of the activity area. On a signal the children may walk, skip, hop, etc., to the music around the activity area. When the music stops the teacher holds up a card. Those children whose cards match the teacher's card run to sit in the chairs. Anyone who gets a seat scores a point. The play resumes. Cards should be exchanged frequently among the children.

Application: This visual discrimination activity can be adapted easily to include increasing complexity of the visual discrimination task as well as how the children move about and the task for scoring points. Visual discrimination tasks might also include shapes, designs, letters (both capital and lower case).

Letter Recognition

Concept: Recognizing Letter of the Alphabet

Activity: Letter Spot

Pieces of paper with lower case letters are placed in various spots around the activity area. There should be several pieces of paper with the same letters. The teacher has a number of large posters with the same but capital letters (An overhead projector may be used to present letters in many letter styles, sizes, and colors). A poster is shown to the class. The children must identify the letter by name and then run to that letter on the floor. Any child who is left without a spot gets a point against him. Any child who has less than five points at the end of the period is considered a winner.

Application: Children are helped to associate letters with their names. After the activity the posters can be put on display around the room.

Concept: Recognizing Letters of the Alphabet

Activity: Call and Catch (variation)

The children stand in a circle. The teacher stands in the center of the circle with a rubber ball. Each child is assigned a different letter. The letter may be written on a card attached to a string which the child wears as a necklace. Each child reads his letter before the activity is started. The teacher calls out a letter and throws the ball into the air. The child who has that letter tries to catch the ball after it bounces. The teacher can provide for individual differences of children. For the slower child the teacher can call the letter and then momentarily hold the ball before throwing it into the air.

Application: This activity provides children the opportunity to become familiar with names and visual identification of letters. Later the teacher could hold up letter cards rather than calling the letter. The children might then have to name the letter and catch the ball. Eventually both upper and lower-case cards might be used in the activity.

Diagnosis of Reading Skills Through Physical Education

As the child moves into the *beginning reading skills*, physical education experiences continue to serve as a valuable means of assessing skill mastery. Skill areas as sight vocabulary, word attack skills, alphabetical order, comprehension, and vocabulary meaning can be developed through various dimensions of physical education experiences. Likewise, level of skill mastery can also be assessed. Activities that utilize the various reading skills mentioned above are described in order to demonstrate the nature of physical education experiences that can be employed.

Sight Vocabulary

Developing sight vocabulary through physical education utilizes words and phrases from materials children are currently reading.

Concept: Sight Vocabulary

Activity: Call Phrase

The children form a circle, facing the center. They may be seated or standing. One child is designated as the caller and stands in the center of the circle. Each child is given a card with a phrase printed on it. Several children can have the same phrase. The caller draws a card from a box containing corresponding phrase cards and holds up the card for everyone to see. When he reads the phrase, this is the signal for those children in the circle with the same phrase to exchange places before the caller can fill in one of the vacant places in the circle. The remaining child becomes the caller.

Application: Children need opportunities to develop quick recognition of phrases. This activity provides the repetition necessary to help children develop familiarity with phrases they are meeting in their reading material. The phrases may be taken from group experience stories, readers, or children's own experience stories.

Word Attack

Word attack skills assessed through physical education experiences may include phonic elements of words, rhyming words, vowel letter patterns, syllables, and endings.

Concept: Auditory Discrimination—Consonant Digraphs (ch, sh, th)

Activity: Mouse and Cheese

A round mousetrap is formed by the children standing in a circle. In the center of the mousetrap is placed the cheese, (a ball or some other object). The children are then assigned one of the consonant digraphs: *sh, ch,* or *th.* When the teacher calls a word beginning with a consonant digraph, all the children with this digraph run around the circle and back to their original place, representing the holes in the trap. Through these original places they run into the circle to get the cheese. The child who gets the cheese is the winning mouse for that turn. Another word is called, and the same procedure is followed. Children may be reassigned digraphs from time to time.

Application: Children need repetition for developing the ability to hear and identify various sound elements within words. This activity enables children to recognize consonant digraphs within the context of whole words. A variation of this activity would be to have the teacher hold up word cards with words beg nning with consonant digraphs rather than saying the word. This variation would provide emphasis on visual discrimination of initial consonant digraphs. Another variation would focus on ending consonant digraphs, either auditory or visual recognition.

Concept: Rhyming Words

Activity: Rhyme Chase

The children form a circle. Each child is given a card with a familiar word from the children's sight vocabulary written on it. The teacher may ask each child to pronounce his word before beginning the activity. The children should then listen and look at the words as each one identifies his word. The teacher then calls out a word that rhymes with one or several of the words held by the children. The child (or children) holds up his rhyming word so all the children see it. He must then give another word that rhymes with his word. This is a signal for all the other children to run to a safety place previously designated by the teacher. The child (or children) with the rhyming words try to tag any one of the other children before he reaches a safe place. A child who is tagged receives a point against him. The object is for the children to get the lowest score possible. Word cards may be exchanged among the children after several turns.

Application: In this activity the children are called upon to relate auditory experiences in rhyming with visual presentations of these words. Sight vocabulary is also emphasized as the children reinforce the concept of visual patterns in rhyming words.

Alphabetical Order

Alphabetizing words is an essential skill for locating words in diction-aries or information in encyclopedias. Physical education experiences utilizing the first two, three, or four letters for alphabetizing can later be developed as the teacher assesses when there is skill mastery of the less difficult tasks of alphabetizing.

Concept: Alphabetical Order

Activity: Alphabet Line-Up

The class is divided into teams. For each team a set of 26 cards, one for each letter of the alphabet, is placed out of order on the chalk tray at the front of the room or pinned to a bulletin board. The teams make rows at a specified distance from the letter display. A goal line is established at the back of the room for each team. The object of the activity is for each member, one at a time, to run to pick up a letter in correct alphabetical order, carry it to the team's goal line, and place the letter side by side in correct order. When each team member has found a letter, the team begins again until the alphabet is complete. The first team to complete placing the alphabet correctly at its goal line wins.

Application: Children need many different types of opportunities to practice putting the letters in correct alphabetical order. This activity provides a new way to practice this skill.

Comprehension

Vocabulary meaning as well as other comprehension skills such as in the following physical education experience utilizing sequence of events can be emphasized in physical education. Sentence Relay further serves as an example of how the buddy system can work in the physical education approach. (*What to Play* and *Changing Seats* are activities presented earlier in the chapter which reinforce vocabulary meaning.)

Concept: Sequence of Events
Activity: Sentence Relay

Relay teams of five children each are selected to make rows before a starting line 10 to 15 feet from sentence charts for each team. The remaining children can serve as scorers. Each child on the team is given a sentence that fits into an overall sequence for the five sentences given each team. (The teams are given duplicate sentences.) Each sentence gives a clue to its position in the sentence sequence, either by idea content or word clue. On a given signal the team members get together and decide the correct sentence order. The child with the first sentence then runs to the sentence chart, places his sentence on the top line of the chart, underlines the key part of the sentence that gives the clue to the sequence, and returns to his team. The child with the next sentence then runs to place his sentence below the first sentence. This procedure continues until the sentences are in order. The team to complete the story with sentences in correct order first wins. The scorers check on the accuracy of the sentence order for each team. For the next game the scorers can exchange places with those who were on the teams. Variations of this activity can include the use of cartoons with each child being given one frame of the cartoon strip. To make the activity more difficult, more sentences may be added to the sequence. To prevent copying, the teacher can give different story sentences to each team.

Application: In this activity those children having difficulty with reading are helped by those who are more able readers and not eliminated from the activity. After the activity is played the teacher should go over key elements in the sentences that provided clues to the proper sequence.

How might Sentence Relay be used for diagnostic purposes? It might be used just as it is described above or certain adaptations might be made. In this case, the reading task in the physical education experience is to recognize key elements in the sentences that provide clues to the proper sequence. The teacher can note whether a child is able to identify appropriate clues to sequence in his sentence. The teacher might observe which children perform the task easily and those who appear to need additional experiences in identifying key elements in sentences relating to sequence.

The activity might also be adapted by changing it to one that utilizes a story with several key sentences missing, the number of missing sentences being the same as the number of children on each team. The reading task would then be one of using context clues of a larger meaning unit to identify the proper order of sentences.

One of the many advantages of the physical education approach is that it is fairly easy for the teacher to identify the specific reading skills being utilized in an activity which in turn facilitates assessment of children's mastery of that skill. In this way diagnostic teaching techniques aid a teacher's effort to adjust the learning activities of the reading program to the needs of the children. The examples presented are representative of almost unlimited possibilities in structuring appropriate reading experiences for children. The creative teacher should be able to develop numerous activities by adapting those presented here to the developmental level and skill needs of the children.

TEACHING READING SKILLS AND CONCEPTS THROUGH PHYSICAL EDUCATION

The physical education experiences in this section of the chapter have been grouped by the major aspects of the reading program. Some of the activities are particularly useful for developing specific language or reading concepts. In these activities the learner acts out the concept and thus is able to visualize as well as get the *feel* of the concept. Other activities help to develop skills by using these skills in highly interesting and stimulating situations.

Suggestions for adapting many of the activities are made in order to extend these types of activities to other elements of the various aspects of the reading program. The activities included have much versatility, depending on the creativeness of teachers and others using them.

Word Analysis Skills

Concept: Recognizing Letters of the Alphabet
Activity: Letter Snatch

The children are divided into two teams of eight to ten each. The teams face each other about ten to twelve feet apart. A small object such as an eraser is placed on the floor between the two teams. The members of both teams are given letters. The teacher then holds up a card with a letter on it. The children from each team who have the letter run out and try to grab the object and return to their line. If the child does so without being tagged by the other child, he scores two points. If he is tagged, the other team scores one point.

Application: Children have the opportunity to practice letter recognition in this activity. Visual matching can be with all small letters at first and then later with all capital letters. After the children have learned both small and capital letters, one team can have small letters and the other capital letters. with the teacher displaying cards showing either type of letter.

Concept: Recognizing Letters of the Alphabet—Matching Capital and Small Letters
Activity: Large and Small

The children are divided into two teams of eight to ten each. The teams stand in lines about 15 feet apart and face in the same direction. The children on the first team are each given a card with a small letter on it. Each member of the second team is given a card with the corresponding capital letters. The members of the first team hold their cards behind them for the second team to be able to see. The teacher touches a child on the second team. This child then runs over to the first team, finds the child with the same letter as his, and tags the child. The child on the first team turns and chases the child who tagged him, who tries to get back into place before the other child touches him. If he is tagged, the first team gets one point; if he gets back safely, team two gets one point. After each child on the second team has had an opportunity to match his letter, the teacher then gives the children on the first team the opportunity to match the letters. To do this, the teams should both face in the opposite direction so that the first team can now see the letters the children on the second team hold behind their backs.

Application: This activity provides the necessary experience in associating capital and small letters that children need to become more familiar with the letters of the alphabet in upper and lower case form.

Concept: Auditory Discrimination—Beginning Sounds of Words

Activity: Match the Sound

A group of eight to ten children form a circle. The children skip around in the circle until the teacher gives a signal to stop. The teacher then says a word and throws a ball directly at one of the children. The teacher begins to count to ten. The child who catches the ball must say another word that begins with the same sound before the teacher counts to ten. If the child does, he gets a point. The child with the most points wins. The other children in the circle must listen carefully to be sure each child calls out a correct word. As the children learn to associate letter names with sounds, the child must not only call another word beginning with the same sound but also must identify the letter that word begins with.

Application: The activity enables children to listen for sounds in the initial position of words. The activity can also be adapted to listening for final position sounds.

Concept: Auditory Discrimination—Consonant Blends

Activity: Crows and Cranes

The playing area is divided by a center line. On opposite ends of the area are drawn base lines, parallel to the center line. The class is divided into two team. The children of one team are designated as Crows and take position on one side of the play area, with the base line on their side of the center line serving as their safety zone. The members of the other team are designated as Cranes and take position on the other side of the play area, with their base line as a safety zone. The teacher stands to one side of the play area by the center line. The teacher then calls out, "Cr-r-anes" or "Cr-r-ows." In calling cranes or crows, the teacher emphasizes the initial consonant blend. If the teacher calls the Crows, they turn and run to their base line to avoid being tagged. The Cranes attempt to tag their opponents before they can cross their base line. The Cranes score a point for each Crow tagged. The Crows and Cranes then return to their places, and the teacher proceeds to call one of the groups; play continues in the same manner. This activity can be extended to include other words beginning with consonant blends, for example, swans and swallow, storks and starlings, squids and squabs.

Application: Repetition of the consonants blends during the activity helps children become aware of these sounds and to develop their auditory perception of the blends in context of words. Discovering names of animals with other consonant blends can help children in their ability to hear consonant blends in the initial position of words.

Concept: Auditory Discrimination—Consonant Blends

Activity: Call Blends

Eight to ten children stand in a circle. The teacher stands in the center of the circle, holding a ball. Each child is assigned an initial consonant blend by the teacher (st, gr, bl, cl, and so forth). When the teacher calls out a word with an initial consonant blend, the ball is thrown into the air. The child assigned that blend must then call a word using the blend and catch the ball after it has bounced once. Depending on the ability level of the children, the teacher can control the amount of time between calling out the blend word and the time the child catches the ball and calls out his word. When the child gives a correct word and catches the ball, he scores one point. The child with the most points wins. The teacher can reassign blends frequently to the children during the activity.

Application: This activity is a supplemental one to reinforce previous auditory and visual presentation of consonant blends in the initial position. Blends used in the activity should be those with which the children have worked. The teacher may write the word on the chalkboard after each time and have the child underline the blend in order to reinforce the blend in the visual context of the word.

Concept: Visual Discrimination—Whole Words

Activity: Cross the Bridge

The activity area is marked off with lines at each end. A child is selected to be the Bridge Keeper. He stands in the center of the area while the remainder of the class stands behind one end line. Each child is given a card with a sight vocabulary word on it. Several children should have the same word. The Bridge Keeper is given a box with a complete set of word cards that correspond to those given the other children and large enough for all children to see. The children call out to the Bridge Keeper, "May we use the bridge? May we use the bridge?" The Bridge Keeper replies, "Yes, if you are this word." He then holds up one of the word cards from his box for all the children to see. The child or children having that word try to cross to the other end line without being tagged by the Bridge Keeper. The procedure is continued again with other words. Those children tagged must help the Bridge Keeper to tag other children as they also try to cross the bridge. Occasionally, the Bridge Keeper may call out, "Everybody across the Bridge," when all the children may run to the opposite end line. The activity can continue until one child remains. He becomes the Bridge Keeper for the next time, or another Bridge Keeper may be selected.

Application: This activity provides children the opportunity to match words visually as a means to reinforce words to the point that they may become a part of the child's sight vocabulary.

Sight Vocabulary

Concept: Sight Vocabulary
Activity: Word Carpet (Variation)

Several squares are drawn on the floor or pieces of paper are placed on the floor to represent Magic Carpets. Each Magic Carpet is numbered one to three to correspond with a numbered list of words on the chalkboard. The words include new vocabulary from the children's experience stories, readers, and social studies or science units. Two teams of children are selected, and each team forms a chain by holding hands. To music, the two teams walk around in circles and back and forth in a zig-zag manner over the Magic Carpets until the music stops. Each child then standing on or closest to a Magic Carpet identifies any word from the numbered list on the board that corresponds with the number at that Magic Carpet. The teacher then erases that word from the list, if it is read correctly. Each team scores one point for any correctly identified word. The team with the highest score wins.

Application: This activity provides an interesting experience whereby new words are given additional emphasis. To focus on meaning of new words, the teacher can require the child who has read a word correctly to put it in a sentence in order for the team to score an additional point. Children can also be helped to identify specific word analysis clues they used to identify their words.

Concept: Sight Vocabulary
Activity: Squirrel and Nut

All the children except one sit at their desks with heads resting on an arm as though sleeping but with one hand out-stretched. The extra child is the Squirrel. The Squirrel who carries a nut (words on cards shaped like a nut), runs quietly about the room and drops a nut into the open hand of a child. The child jumps up from his seat, pronounces the word, and chases the Squirrel, who is safe only when he reaches his nest (seat). The activity continues with the teacher or a child selecting a new Squirrel.

Application: Words selected for the activity may come from experience stories and stories read on that or the previous day. These kinds of activities provide the necessary repetition to develop instant recognition of words and can be used to maintain words in addition to word banks and word games that the children utilize in the classroom.

Comprehension

Concept: Following Directions
Activity: Simon Says

The children stand about the activity area facing the person who plays Simon. Every time Simon says to do something, the children must do it. However, if a command is given without the prefix "Simon says," the children must remain motionless. For example, when "Simon says take two steps," everyone must take two steps. But if Simon says, "Walk backward two steps," no one should move. If a child moves at the wrong time or turns in the wrong direction, the child puts one hand on his head. The second time he misses, he puts the other hand on his head. The more quickly the commands are given and the greater number of commands, the more difficult the activity will be. The child with the lower score wins with points scored when a wrong movement is made.

Application: This activity provides children the opportunity to follow oral directions in a highly motivating situation. The rules of the activity, as adapted, allow those children who need the practice additional chances even if they have points scored against them.

Concept: Following Directions
Activity: Do This, Do That

Flash cards of "Do This" and "Do That" are used in this activity. One child is selected to be the leader and stands in front of the group. The teacher holds up a flash card, and the leader makes a movement such as walking in place, running in place, swinging the arms, or hopping up and down on one foot. The children follow the actions of the leader when the sign says "Do This." When the teacher holds up the sign "Do That," the children must not move although the leader continues the action. A point is scored against a child who is caught moving. The leader can be changed frequently.

Application: This activity can be used to help children to read carefully in order to follow directions. Later, the activity can be adapted by having the leader display written directions on flash cards, for example, hop in place, jump once, walk in place, and the like.

Concept: Classification

Activity: Ducks Fly

Children stand at their seats. One of them may be the leader. At the first-grade level it might, in some cases, be better for the teacher to be the leader. The leader faces the class. He names different things that can fly, as ducks, birds, and airplanes. As the leader call out "Ducks fly, Birds fly, Airplanes fly," he moves his arms as if flying. The class follows as long as he names something that can fly. If he says "Elephants fly," and although the leader continues to keep his arms moving as if flying, the children must stop moving their arms. Those who are caught flying have a point scored against them. If the arms get tired, the leader might try things that walk, swim, and so forth, and the children then make the appropriate movement. The child with the lowest score wins.

Application: Children need to develop the skill of classifying things into groups having common characteristics. Children should be helped to notice that some animals actually can do several of the movements named as flying, walking, and/or swimming. Later, children can collect pictures of animals and make a display of animals who walk, swim, and the like.

Concept: Vocabulary Meaning—Colors

Activity: Rainbow

The children form a circle, facing the center. The children may be seated or standing. One child is designated the Caller and stands in the center of the circle. Instead of counting off by numbers, the children are given small pieces of paper of one of the basic colors. The Caller is given a set of word cards, one for each of the basic colors corresponding to the colors given the children in the circle. The Caller selects one word card and shows it. The children with this color attempt to change places while the Caller tries to get to one of the vacant places in the circle. The remaining child can become the new Caller or a Caller can be selected by the teacher or children. The Caller may show two word cards. Those children with the two colors then run to change places with the Caller again trying to get to one of the vacant places in the circle. At any time the Caller or teacher may call out "Rainbow." When this call is given, everyone must change to a different position.

Application: Children need many opportunities to develop their recognition of words in activities of this nature in which they are associating the word with the concept the word represents. This activity can be simplified in order for it to become appropriate for a language development activity. The Caller can have just color cards matching those of the children. Later, when children have learned to match colors, the Caller can call out the names of the colors.

Concept: Vocabulary Meaning—Over and Under

Activity: Over and Under Relay

The children are divided into several teams. They stand one behind the other, separated about one foot apart. A ball is given to the first child on each team, who stands at the head of the row. On a signal he passes the ball behind him over his head and calls "over." The second child in the row takes the ball and passes it between his legs and calls "under." Number three in the row takes and passes the ball over his head and calls "over" and so on down the row until the last one receives the ball. He then runs to the head of the row and starts passing the ball back in the same manner. The team whose first person reaches the head of the row first wins.

Application: This activity helps children to dramatize the meaning of the words *over* and *under*. For a variation the teacher can hold up a card with either *over* or *under* written on it to indicate how the ball should be passed by the child moving forward to the front of the team.

Concept: Vocabulary Meaning—Word Opposites

Activity: Word Change

The class is divided into two teams who line up at opposite ends of the activity area. Each child is given a word printed on a card. The words given to one team are the word opposites of the words given to the other team. One child is selected to be *It* and stands in the middle of the activity area. The teacher calls out a word, and this word and its opposite run and try to exchange places. *It* attempts to get into one of the vacated places before the two children can exchange places. The remaining child can become *It* for the next time or a new *It* can be chosen.

Application: This activity focuses on the meaning of sight vocabulary words. It can be varied with emphasis on synonyms, with teams given words that are similar in meaning.

The examples presented are representative of almost unlimited possibilities in structuring reading learning experiences for children through physical education activities. The creative teacher should be able to develop numerous other activities by adapting those presented here to the developmental skill needs of the children.

PHYSICAL EDUCATION READING CONTENT

The term *reading content* is easy to describe because it is simply concerned with the information that a given reading selection contains. Therefore, physical education reading content provides for reading material that is oriented to physical education situations. Stories of different lengths are prepared for various readability levels, and the content focuses upon any aspect of physical education. Concent can be concerned with such forms of physical education as active games, rhythmic activities and self-testing activities.

Physical education reading content—at least as conceived here—is concerned with my work which originally involved the preparation of a number of physical education-oriented stories. These stories were used with several hundred children, and on the basis of the findings of my studies, the following generalizations have been derived.

1. When a child is self-motivated and interested, he reads. In this case the reading was done without the usual motivating devices such as pictures, clues, and illustrations.
2. These physical education stories were found to be extremely successful in stimulating interest in reading and at the same time improving the child's ability to read.
3. Because the material for these physical education stories was scientifically selected, prepared, and tested, it is unique in the field of children's independent reading material. The outcomes have been most satisfactory in terms of children's interest in reading content of this nature as well as motivation to read.

From Listening to Reading

Before getting directly into the *use* of physical education reading content, I want to take into account the important relationship between listening and reading. An important thing to remember is that the comprehension skills for listening are the same as the comprehension skills for reading (see inventory of comprehension skills presented later). The essential difference in these two receptive phases of language is in the form of *input* that is used. That is, listening is dependent upon the *auditory* sense and reading is dependent upon the *visual* sense. Since the main goal of reading is comprehension, it is important to recognize that as children listen to physical education situations and react to them, they are developing essential skills for reading.

This brings us to the important question: "Should we read to children?" People who spend their time studying about this reply with an unqualified affirmative. That is, there seems to be solid evidence to support the idea that reading to children improves their vocabulary knowledge, reading comprehension, interest in reading, and the general quality of language development. This is emphasized at this point because we shall see later that reading to children is an important dimension in the use of physical education reading content.

The AMAV Technique

My procedure for learning to read through the use of physical education reading content is identified as the *AMAV Technique,* some examples of which will be presented later. The AMAV Technique involves a learning sequence of *auditory input* to *movement* to *auditory-visual input,* as depicted in the following diagram.

$$A\text{uditory} \rightarrow M\text{ovement} \rightarrow A\text{uditory-Visual}$$

Essentially, this technique is a procedure for working through a physical education experience to develop comprehension, first in listening and then in reading. The A → M aspect of AMAV is a directed listening-thinking activity. The child first receives the thoughts and feelings expressed in the physical education story through the auditory sense by listening to the story read by the teacher. Following this, the child, or children, engages in the physical education experience inherent in the story, and thereby demonstrates understanding of and reaction to the story. By engaging in the physical education experience, the development of comprehension becomes a part of the child's *physical reality.*

After the physical education experience in the directed listening-thinking activity, the child, or children, moves to the final aspect of the AMAV Technique (A–V), a combination of auditory and visual experience by listening to the story read by the teacher and *reading along* with the teacher. In this manner, comprehension is brought to the reading experience.

Although the sequence of listening to reading is a natural one, bridging the gap to the point of handling the verbal symbols required in reading poses various problems for many children. One of the outstanding features of the AMAV Technique is that the physical education experience helps to serve as a bridge between listening and reading by providing direct purposeful experience for the child through the physical education experience after listening to the story. (See the following diagram.)

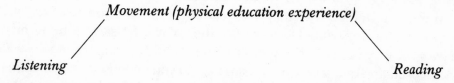

The following is a specific suggestion for procedures that might be utilized in working with physical education stories. In this situation during which the children are taking turns acting out their favorite stunt story the teacher might direct the following discussion after a child's presentation of *George Giraffe*.

George Giraffe

There is a tall animal in a far away land.
He has a long neck.
His name is George Giraffe
You could look like him if you did this.
Place your arms high over your head.
Put your hands together.
Point them to the front.
This will be his neck and head.
Now walk like George Giraffe.
This is how.
Stand on your toes.
Walk with your legs straight.
    Could you walk so you would look like George Giraffe?

TEACHER: Wasn't that an interesting way Johnny showed us how George Giraffe looked? (Children) What di you think George Giraffe looked like from what Johnny did? (Children) What did Johnny do to look like George Giraffe? What did Johnny do to have a long neck like George Giraffe? (Children) Can someone else make a long neck? (Children demonstrate.) Oh, you are *all* very good at making long necks. Particularly Jimmy. How did Johnny walk to be like George Giraffe? Can someone show us? (Children demonstrate.) What do you have to do to walk like George Giraffe? (Children) Is it easy to pretend to be a giraffe? Let's try it and find out. (All children demonstrate). Did you feel awkward? (Children) We often say that giraffes look ungainly or awkward. Do you think these are good words to describe a giraffe? (Children) Can you think of other animals that also look awkward or ungainly? (Children) That was good, Johnny. You really showed us how to look like a giraffe. You must have read the story very carefully. Bobby, you said you had also read the story about George Giraffe. Why do I say, "Johnny must have read very carefully?" (Bobby) That's right. It is important to use all the information that the story gives us to help you pretend to be something. That was fun, wasn't it? (Children) All right. Now Mary is going to tell us about her story. But this time we are going to do it differently. This time Mary is *not* going to tell us the name of her story, or what she is pretending to be. We will have to guess *who* or *what* she is. (In this manner the group continues to share, discuss, act out, and evaluate the stories the children present.)

This story has been written about a self-testing activity (stunt). The two stories that follow have been written about a rhythmic activity and an active game.

Our Song and Dance

Here is a new dance.
You can enjoy it with your friends.
First, sing the words of the dance to the tune of
　　"London Bridge."
Now, stand in two lines facing your partner.
As you sing the words, do the dance steps.
Here are the words for your song and dance.

　　Bow to partner.
　　Tap right toe.
　　Tap right toe.
　　Tap right toe.
　　Bow to partner.
　　Tap right toe.
　　My dance partner.
　　Bow to partner.
　　Slide to right.
　　Slide to right.
　　Slide to right.

Bow to partner.
Slide to right.
My dance partner.
Bow to partner.
Tap left toe.
Tap left toe.
Tap left toe.
Bow to partner.
Tap left toe.
My dance partner.
Bow to partner.
Slide to left.
Slide to left.
Slide to left.
Bow to partner.
Slide to left.
My dance partner.

Could you do this dance with your friend?

Sparky Sparrow Plays A Game

The birds are asleep in their nests.
Sparky Sparrow does not have a nest.
He says, "I will have some fun."
He calls, "Fly!"
Each bird flies to another nest.
Sparky finds a nest.
One bird is left out.
He calls, "Fly!"
Again the birds find other nests.
They have fun.

Could you show other children how to play Sparky Sparrow's game?

Other examples of physical education reading content are given in Chapters 6 and 7 in the form of mathematics physical education stories and science physical education stories.

Inventory of Listening and/or Reading Comprehension Skills
Directions: Check YES or NO to indicate proficiency or lack of proficiency with which the child is using skills.

SKILLS

Yes   *No*

_____ _____ 1. Getting Facts—Does the child understand what to do and how to do it?

_____ _____ 2. Selecting Main Idea—Does the child use succinct instructions in preparing for and doing the physical education activity?

_____ _____ 3. Organizing Main Ideas by Enumeration and Sequence—Does the child know the order in which the activity is performed?

_____ _____ 4. Following Directions—Does the child proceed with the activity according to the precise instructions in the story?

_____ _____ 5. Drawing Inferences—Does the child seem to draw reasonable conclusions as shown by the way he imitates the animal, person, or object in the story?

_____ _____ 6. Gaining Independence in Word Mastery—Does the child use word analysis to get a word without asking for help? (This applies only if child has been introduced to word analysis skills.)

_____ _____ 7. Building a Meaningful Vocabulary—Does the child use any of the words in the story in his speaking vocabulary as he proceeds in the physical education experience?

_____ _____ 8. Distinguishing Fact from Fantasy—Does the child indicate which stories are real and which are imaginary, particularly as far as some of the characters are concerned?

It should be recognized that different children will develop comprehension skills at different rates. Therefore, one should be patient and provide cheerful guidance as needed in assisting the child in performing the physical education experiences depicted in the stories.

Guidelines for Teachers in Preparing Physical Education Stories

It is likely that some teachers will want to try to develop some of their own physical education reading content, and I heartily recommend that they try their hand at it. Should this be the case, the following guidelines are submitted for consideration.

1. In general, the *new* word load should be kept relatively low.
2. When new words are used, there should be as much repetition of these words as possible and appropriate.
3. Sentence length and lack of complex sentences should be considered in keeping the level of difficulty of material within the ability level of children.
4. Consideration should also be given to the reading values and literary merits of a story. Using a character or characters in a story setting helps to develop interest.
5. The activity to be used in the story should *not* be readily identifiable. When children identify an activity early in the story, there can be resulting minimum attention on their part to get the necessary details to engage in the physical education experience. Thus, in developing a physical education story, it is important that the nature of the activity and procedures for it unfold gradually.

In closing this chapter let me say that I have attempted to show many possibilities available for the integration of physical education and reading. Perhaps these examples will be of use to teachers and also inspire them to develop many additional activities on their own.

Chapter 5

INTEGRATION OF PHYSICAL EDUCATION AND THE OTHER LANGUAGE ARTS

One of the very important elementary school curriculum areas is the *language arts* program. This program includes listening, speaking, reading, and writing, all of which are concerned with communication. The primary purpose of the language arts program in the modern elementary school is to facilitate communication.

Speaking and writing can be referred to as the *expressive* phases of language, while listening and reading are considered the *receptive* phases. This implies that through speaking and writing the individual has the opportunity to express his or her own thoughts and feelings to others. Through reading and listening the individual receives the thoughts and feelings of others.

Although it has been indicated that the language arts program contains listening, speaking, reading, and writing, the reader should not interpret this to mean that these are considered as entirely separate entities. On the contrary, they are closely interrelated, and each can be considered a component part of the broad area of communication. Such areas of study in the elementary school as spelling, word meanings, and word recognition are involved in each of the four areas.

The importance of the interrelationship of the various language arts can be shown in different ways. For example, children must use words in speaking and have them meaningful before they can read them successfully. Also, they can spell better the words that they read with understanding and that they want to use for their own purpose. In addition, their handwriting even improves when they use it in purposeful and meaning- ful communication when someone they like is going to read it. Perhaps the two most closely interrelated and interdependent phases of language arts are listening and reading. In fact, as mentioned in the previous chapter, most reading specialists agree that learning to listen is the first step in learning to read.

The modern elementary school gives a great deal of attention to this interrelationship of the various phases of the language arts. This is reflected in the way in which language experiences are being provided for children in the better-than-average elementary school. In the traditional elementary school it was a common practice to treat such aspects of the language arts as reading, writing, and spelling as separate subjects. As a result, they became more or less isolated and unrelated entities, and their full potential as media of expression probably was never fully realized. In the modern elementary school, where children have more freedom of expression and consequently, greater opportunity for self-expression, the approach to teaching language arts is one that relates the various language areas to particular areas of interest. All of the phases of language arts—listening, speaking, reading, and writing—are thus used in the solution of problems in all curriculum areas. This procedure is primarily based upon the assumption that skill in communication should be developed in all of the activities engaged in by children.

LANGUAGE ARTS EXPERIENCES THROUGH PHYSICAL EDUCATION

Inasmuch as elementary school physical education predominantly involves gross body movement, one might think that there would be few opportunities for language expression and reception. On the contrary, there exists a rather wide variety of such opportunities. Not only are the various language arts areas essential to the most desirable physical education teaching-learning situation, but there are numerous ways in which physical education and language arts can complement each other in the reciprocal development of skills, understandings, and appreciations.

Every facet of life has its own vocabulary, and the "language" of physical education is one that is widely used in American life. Many of us have used, at one time or another, the expression "that's the way the ball bounces" to refer to a situation in which the outcome was not as desirable as was anticipated. Or, "that's par for the course," meaning that the difficulty was anticipated and the results were no better or no worse than expected. When we are "home free" we tend to refer to having gotten out of a tight situation, with results better than expected. The expression "the bases are loaded" describes a situation in which a critical point has been reached and there is much at stake on the next event or series of events. If you have "two strikes against you," you are operating at a grave disadvantage, and if someone "strikes out," he has failed.

It is possibly that some foreign words will be introduced to children for the first time through folk dances. In some cases teachers make lists of vocabulary words that grow out of various kinds of physical education experiences.

Since *reading* has been dealt with in a separate chapter, the following discussions will be concerned with the areas of *listening, speaking,* and *writing.*

LISTENING EXPERIENCES
THROUGH PHYSICAL EDUCATION

Listening is more than just hearing. It also involves a critical analysis of what is actually heard. Various research studies indicate that listening is the most-used of the language arts, and it has been found that the median of school time that elementary school children spend in listening is upwards of 60 percent. In some cases teachers have estimated that children are "learning by listening" about 75 minutes per day. It is interesting to note that some observations have shown that this estimate could be over 160 minutes per day.

In spite of the fact that listening is the most used of the language arts, it is perhaps the most neglected of all of the communication skills. This paradoxical situation has probably been brought on by the traditional type of thinking that held that children came to school to listen and that they were endowed to do so without any training in this particular skill. At the present time many educators feel that critical listening should be taught at all of the educational grade levels. The implementation of this theory does not appear to be entirely compatible with current practice. For example, in a recent examination of over 200 language arts curriculum bulletins, I found that in only about 40 percent of them was listening given an important place, and it was not even mentioned in almost 30 percent of the bulletins.

The nature of physical education is such that children will perhaps not be required to do as much listening as they will in some of the other curriculum areas. However, it is extremely important, when physical education is taught, that teachers give a great deal of consideration to the importance of listening as a receptive communication skill. This consideration can be dealt with in a least two different ways. First, it is necessary to consider the actual listening possibilities involved in the physical education teaching-learning situation. And second, teachers should be aware of those physical education activities that involve opportunities for the use of skill in listening. As far as the physical education teaching-learning situation is concerned, the *auditory-input* phase and the *evaluation* phase of teaching provide an opportunity for teachers to help children to become more effective listeners. In this particular connection, it is suggested that the reader refer back to these two phases discussed in Chapter 2.

As a general rule, listening is not taught as a separate curriculum area, and, as pointed out previously, it is not always given a place of importance in the elementary school curriculum. Because of this situation, perhaps all of the curriculum areas should contribute in one way or another to the development of this skill. Herein lies the second way that teachers can give consideration to listening as it applies to physical education. In other words, how can the area of physical education contribute satisfactorily to the development of listening skills in elementary school children? It should perhaps be mentioned that physical education can make a very fine contribution to skill in listening due to the fact that children are motivated to listen because of their inherent interest in most of the activities of this particular curriculum area. In fact, scores of my observations have shown that children are much more attentive during the auditory-input phase of a physical education lesson than is the case in most other curriculum areas.

There are certain types of physical education activities that require critical listening in order that there may be successful participation in these activities. Sometimes in the evaluation phase of a physical education lesson, awareness of children to the importance of listening in a certain activity is evidenced by such statements as "We need to listen better" or "We have to listen to be good at this game." Some general conditions in which listening is essential to satisfactory performance of the activity include (1) listening to musical accompaniment to identify mood and tempo, (2) listening to calls for various types of dances, such as square dances, (3) listening to directions from teammates during the course of a game, and (4) listening for starting and stopping signals.

In some cases teachers can capitalize upon opportunities to help children become more effective listeners by emphasizing the possibilities for listening that are inherent in some physical education activities. The practical example of a simulated teaching-learning situation that follows is illustrative of this particular technique.

The procedure shows how the game Crows and Cranes can be satisfactorily used as a listening exercise for initial consonant blends with a class of second grade children. (This activity was described in Chapter 4.)

TEACHER: Boys and girls, today we are going to learn a new game, but first I want to see how well you can listen, because you must listen closely in the game we are going to play. Now listen closely. I am going to say two sentences and I am going to leave one word out of each sentence. I will tell you the sound with which the word begins. You are to use that sound and the meaning of the other words to decide what word I leave out. Does everyone understand? Fine, let's begin. The word I am going to leave out of the first sentence begins with the same sound as cream, crows, and cranes. Now listen. The little boy was so unhappy that he began to (*pause*). What word did I leave out?

CHILD: I know. The boy began to cry.

TEACHER: That's right the word was cry. Now let's try the second one. Children like to eat ice (*pause*) cones. What was the word that time?

CHILD: That's easy! Cream.

TEACHER: Fine. Now the new game we are going to play is one in which we will use the new sound that we have learned. The name of the game is Crows and Cranes and the new sound is "cr." Get into the same groups we were in the other day for the game Hill Dill. Bring your lines close together. This side will be the Crows and this side will be the Cranes. We will use the same goals that we used for Hill Dill. I will call out either Crows or Cranes. If I call Crows, all of the Crows will turn and run to the goal and the Cranes will try to tag as many as they can. If I call Cranes, the Crows will chase the Cranes in the same way. Now we will have to listen closely for the new sound. Are you ready?

(Children participate in the game for a specified amount of time and then the teacher evaluates the activity with them.)

TEACHER: You seemed to have fun playing Crows and Cranes. What were some of the things you like about it?

CHILD: I like to run.

CHILD: I like to chase and tag.

CHILD: I caught two at once.

TEACHER: Yes, there were many things that you liked about it. What do we have to do in order to be good at this game?

CHILD: Well, for one thing, you have to be able to run fast.

CHILD: You have to listen so you know when to run.

TEACHER: If we played it again, can you think of any ways to make it a better game? Should we always use the words "Crows and Cranes"?

CHILD: We could change the words.

TEACHER: How do you mean, George?

CHILD: Maybe we could use other words that begin with the same two letters. Say, like "grey and green."

TEACHER: I think that is a splendid idea. We will try the game again tomorrow and I would like to have you think of as many words as you can that we might use in this game.

Another very important way to improve upon listening skills through physical education is to provide activities that can help children with *auditory perception*. Incidentally, several activities of this nature were presented in Chapter 4. These activities which provided for *auditory discrimination* were: Man from Mars, Mouse and Cheese, Match the Sound, Crows and Cranes, and Call Blends. Following are several additional activities that can be useful in improving auditory perception and thus facilitate a child's ability to listen.

I Say Stoop

The teacher or a child acting as the leader stands in front of the group which has formed a line. The leader says either, "I say stoop" or "I say stand." The leader carries out actions, but the class must carry out the commands rather than his actions. For example, if he says "I say stand" and he stoops, all of the children who failed to follow the command but follow the action, would have a point scored against them. Many opposite action or direction words could be used, such as: stop and go, run and walk, up and down, forward and backward, and so forth. If the leader cannot think of two words, or if there are no specific words that need attention, the teacher can whisper those words to the leader.

Comment: This activity not only provides for alertness in auditory-motor association, but also can give practice in recognizing word opposites.

Boiling Water

Two or more circles are formed. Each circle is given one or more balls. A container such as a wastebasket is set along the sidelines of the activity area. One child in each circle is the leader. When the teacher calls "cold water," the children in each circle *pass* the ball from one child to the next. Whenever the teacher calls "warm water," the children *roll* the ball across the center of the circle from one to another. If the teacher calls "boiling water," the children *throw* the ball to different ones in the circle. When the teacher calls "water vapor," the ball is immediately thrown to the circle leader who then runs with it to the container on the sidelines. The team whose leader reaches the container first wins.

Comment: This game can be used as a diagnostic technique to help determine how well children can discern auditory cues and perform the action required.

Dog Chase

The class is divided into five or six groups. The members of each group are given the name of a dog, such as collie, poodle, and so on. The small groups then mingle into one large group. One child, acting as the leader, throws a ball or other object away from the groups, at the same time calling out one of the dog names. All of the children with this dog name run after the object. The one who gets possession of it first becomes the leader for the next time.

Comment: The teacher can use this activity as a diagnostic technique by observing those children who react slowly or do not react at all to the auditory input.

Cowboys and Indians

The class is divided into two equal groups. One group is the Cowboys and the other the Indians. Each group stands on a goal line at opposite ends of the activity area. Both groups face in the same direction. To start the game the Cowboys creep up behind the Indians as quietly as possible. The Indians listen for the Cowboys, and when it is determined from the sound that they are near, one person who has been previously designated calls out, "The Cowboys are coming!" The Indians then turn and try to tag as many Cowboys as they can before they reach their own goal line. Those caught become members of the opposite group. The above procedure is reversed and the game continues.

Comment: The children must listen carefully because the sounds can be high or low or soft and loud.

Detective

One child is chosen to take the part of the Detective. He leaves the room while the rest of the class members decide upon a child who will be the "victim." The victim has something about him changed such as taking a shoe lace out of a shoe, putting his sweater on backwards, or the like. The Detective then returns to the room and starts to look for the victim. The children in the class clap softly, and when the Detective gets closer to the victim the clapping becomes louder. The Detective tries to identify the victim and the change that has been made. The game proceeds with the selection of a new Detective.

Comment: Children have the opportunity to recognize differences and to recognize soft and loud tones.

Merry Circle

The children form a circle. An object, such as a beanbag, ball, or eraser, is placed in the center of the circle. The children count off by fours. The first child is number 1; the second, 2; the third, 3; the fourth, 4; and the next child is number 1, and so on. The number 1s are given a card with the letters "ch" on it, the 2s a "sh" card, the 3s a "th" card, and the 4s a "wh" card. The players face counterclockwise. The teacher calls out a word that begins with any one of the consonants on the cards that the children have. For example, if the teacher called out the word "this," all the children holding "th" cards (in this case the number 3s) would run around the outside of the circle and back to their own place and into the center to touch the object. The child touching the object first is declared the winner. The teacher calls out various words and the game proceeds.

Comment: This activity requires listening and associating the sound of a consonant blend with the form.

Rhyme Game

The children form a circle, and one child is selected to be *It* and stands in the center of the circle. The children in the circle are given a small card with a word written on it. *It* points to a child in the circle and this child must give a word which rhymes with the word he has on his card. He holds his card up so all of the other children can see it. When he gives a rhyming word, that is the signal for all of the children to run to a safety place previously designated by the teacher. (Safety may be wood, metal, or the like.) The child gives chase and attempts to tag any of the children before a safe place is reached. If tagged, a child becomes *It* and the game proceeds as before.

Comment: This activity provides an opportunity for listening for and recognizing likenesses and differences in sounds of words, especially rhyming words.

Fundamental Rhythms

The children interpret music or other accompaniment through body movement in such fundamental rhythmic activities as walking, running, stopping, rising, falling, bending, stretching, galloping, skipping, and the like. Any type of satisfactory accompaniment may be used that will "tell" children the difference between one rhythm and another.

Comment: This activity requires listening to develop an understanding of accent. The child listens for sounds that are high or low, or soft or loud.

Shoemaker's Dance

In this activity sing the following verse, with the accompanying actions.

Wind, wind, wind your thread	(Roll hands over each other three times.)
Wind, wind, wind your thread.	(Reverse by rolling opposite direction.)
Pull, pull. Tap, tap, tap.	(Pulling and pounding motion.)
Wind, wind, wind your thread.	(Couples join hands and skip, run,
Wind, wind, wind your thread.	walk or gallop around the circle.
Pull, pull. Tap, tap, tap.	Children can change fundamental rhythmic pattern while keeping time to the accompaniment.)

Comment: Auditory discrimination can be developed by listening for changes in rhythmical pattern and showing change through motion.

Puppy Dog Walk

The children form a circle and walk around on all fours with knees bent. During this time the teacher calls out words with the same beginning sounds such as "ball-bird-big." If she calls a word with a different beginning sound, all of the children stand and continue walking upright. When the teacher begins the words with the same beginning sound, they continue as before. This activity can be varied by using any beginning or ending sounds, or consonant blends.

Comment: There is the opportunity to develop auditory discrimination in beginning or ending sounds of words.

Blackboard Relays

There are a number of variations of blackboard relays that can be performed. Examples include (1) The first person writes a word on the board called out by the teacher, the second person puts the first letter of this word's opposite on the board, the third person puts on the second letter, and so on, until the word is completed. If the word called is "wrong" the first person would put the letter "r" on the board for the word "right." (2) The teacher reads a sentence that uses a word that is a homonym (right or write). The children run to the board and put down the proper word which fits the context meaning. (3) The teacher gives an initial consonant blend, such as "cr," "bl," or the like. Each child goes to the board and writes down a word with the same initial blend.
Comment: This activity can extend the knowledge of opposites. What a word means depends upon how it is used with the words around it in a sentence (auditory perception of homonyms).

Gossip

The class is divided into a number of team rows. The leader of each row whispers a sentence to the second person and this procedure is continued until the last person has received the message. He runs to a designated point where the teacher is standing, and gives her the message. A new message is given and the game proceeds until all have had an opportunity to carry a message.
Comment: This activity provides an opportunity to develop accuracy in listening and speaking as well.

In the Manner

One person is selected as *It* and goes to the far end of the activity area. The rest of the children station themselves on a starting line at the other end of the activity area. They decide upon a word and they approach *It.* When they get close to *It,* they begin to do things "in the manner" of the word selected. For example, if the word selected is "quickly," they may do a number of things in a quick manner. They might move "quickly," talk "quickly," and the like. When *It* guesses the word he gives chase to the players, who try to get to the starting line before being tagged. All of those tagged become helpers for the next time. (Various parts of speech may be used and word endings, such as "ly," "ing," "es," and "est," may be emphasized.)

Comment: The children must listen carefully to recognize parts of speech and word endings.

SPEAKING EXPERIENCES THROUGH PHYSICAL EDUCATION

The term *speaking* as used here implies any form of oral expression. Speaking is the second most used of the language arts and is surpassed only by listening in terms of the percentage of time that elementary school children spend in using the various facets of the language arts. When considered in these terms, the old adage, "Children should be seen and not heard," should be a part of "vanishing America" as far as the modern elementary school is concerned. It is a well-known fact that the present-day elementary school tends to place a great deal of emphasis upon freedom of expression of children. Consequently, it seems logical to assume that considerable attention should be given to ways and means of improving oral expression among children. However, in spite of the significance that educators place upon the medium of oral expression, it has perhaps not occupied the place of importance in the elementary school curriculum enjoyed by some of the more traditional curriculum areas. Undoubtedly, in a good many cases it will be the task of teachers to develop and improve skill in oral expression by using it to best advantage in the other curriculum areas. In this regard, it will be the purpose here to explore some ways in which physical education can contribute satisfactorily to the development and improvement of oral expression among elementary school children.

Before discussing some of the ways in which physical education can be integrated with the area of oral expression, it should be mentioned that it is possible in some cases for physical education experiences to detract from, rather than contribute to, proper oral expression. For example, some physical education experiences are organized and conducted in such a way that children are not given an opportunity to express themselves orally other than by the sort of meaningless shouting that occurs during a game. This statement should not be interpreted to mean that children should refrain from talking, shouting, laughing, and otherwise fully enjoying their physical education experiences. On the other hand, it does mean that while this form of expression is most desirable, it should not be falsely classified as meaningful oral communication.

The suggestions that follow are indicative of some of the possible ways in which physical education experiences can satisfactorily contribute to worthwhile oral expression.

1. Some activities, such as square dancing, require that instructions be given during the activity. When children are given opportunities to do some of the "calling" for dance activities, oral expression and good enunciation become an important factor in the success of the activity.
2. In the evaluation phase of a physical education lesson, children have a fine opportunity for meaningful oral expression if the evaluation is skillfully guided by the teacher.
3. Sometimes teachers may assign children to "look up" a game for the purpose of explaining to the other children in the class how the game is played. This procedure can be followed when committees of children are assigned to explore the recreational activities of people of a particular country or of a given historical period.
4. Oral reading is a form of speaking and as such it can be used to improve oral expression. This procedure can take place by lettering directions for an activity on a chart and having one or more children read the instructions aloud while other children demonstrate. An example of this procedure is the case of a fourth grade class learning the dance *Dixieland.* The following is a facsimile of the lettered chart from which directions were read by children:

HOW TO DANCE DIXIELAND

FORMATION: COUPLES IN A DOUBLE CIRCLE, PARTNERS SIDE BY SIDE, INSIDE HANDS ARE JOINED AND ALL FACE COUNTERCLOCKWISE.

STEP I.   A. STARTING WITH THE OUTSIDE FOOT, WALK THREE STEPS FORWARD AND POINT INSIDE TOE. REPEAT, STARTING WITH THE INSIDE FOOT.

B. GIRL TURNS IN PLACE UNDER BOY'S ARM WITH FOUR RUNNING STEPS. BOY TURNS UNDER GIRL'S ARM THE SAME WAY.

STEP II. PARTNERS FACE EACH OTHER AND JOIN BOTH HANDS WITH ARMS EXTENDED SIDEWARD AT SHOULDER HEIGHT. EIGHT SLIDES AROUND CIRCLE COUNTERCLOCKWISE. EIGHT SLIDES

AROUND CIRCLE CLOCKWISE. REPEAT STEPS I
AND II AS THE MUSIC PROCEEDS.

5. There are some cases in which oral expression is a very important
part of the activity and as such becomes essential to its success. An
example of such an activity is a game called *Warning the Settlers.* In
the following description of this game, the obvious importance of
oral expression is evident. The class is divided into four or five
columns, with an equal number of children standing one behind
the other in each column. (With large classes more columns should
be formed.) One child is selected from each column to serve as
captain or "first messenger." He takes a position at a distance
approximately 50 to 100 feet from his column. Each of these children,
the first messengers, is given an identical secret message on a card.
For example, the message on each child's card might read: "Indian
uprising! Meet before the moon rises tonight just south of Martin's
Hill." After each of the first messengers has read the message on his
card and knows what it says, he runs from his starting point to the
place where his team is waiting. He brings back the first child
(second messenger) in his column, leading him by the hand and
telling him the message as they run. The first child returns for the
second child and so on until each member of the team is in position
behind his captain. It is important that each messenger express the
message clearly as it is relayed because the winning team will be
determined by how nearly right the last messenger is able to give
the message to the teacher. For example, if a team finishes first in
the running, it would also have to have the message most nearly
correct in order to gain first place. This activity is well suited for
integration with a social studies unit on Western expansion in
developing an understanding of how the pioneers defended their
homes. It can be pointed out by the teacher that in this particular
case good oral expression could be the determining factor in protection and safety of a particular group of people.

The simulated teaching-learning situation which follows is intended
to point out more clearly to the reader how a game involving oral
expression can be used satisfactorily in a practical teaching situation.
The name of the game is *Have You Seen My Sheep?*

The players may stand or be seated in a circle. One player is selected
to be *It* to act as a "farmer" or a "shepherd." He walks around the outside

of the circle, stops behind one of the children, and asks, "Have you seen my sheep?" The child responds by asking, "What does your sheep look like?" *It* then describes another player in the circle while the second child tries to determine who is being described. As soon as he finds out from the description who the described player is, he chases that individual around the outside of the circle, trying to tag him before he can run around the circle and return to his place. If the player is tagged, he becomes *It.* If he is not tagged, the chaser is *It* and the game is repeated. The original *It* does not take part in this chase, but steps into the circle in the space vacated by the chaser. If the game is played in the classroom, the children may sit at their seats. The person described runs for safety to a designated empty seat. The person who was *It* goes back to his own seat.

TEACHER: In reading we have learned that some words look alike, and some have small differences. Each boy and girl looks like some other one in one way or another, but each has an individual look that makes him or her different from anyone else. Do you think you would recognize yourself if I described you?

CHILD: If you said a boy with red hair, I would know who it is.

TEACHER: That would be easy because Frank is the only boy with red hair in our class. Do you think you could describe someone else so that we could recognize him or her?

CHILD: Can I try first?

TEACHER: We can play a game where we can see if we can describe others and also recognize ourselves when we are described. The game is called Have You Seen My Sheep? Will you make a circle? Fred, let's make believe that you are a farmer and that you have lost one of your sheep. You will walk around the circle and tap someone on the back. Then you will say to that person "Have you seen my sheep?" The person that you tap will ask, "What does your sheep look like?" You will then tell this person what your sheep looks like, describing one of the children in the circle. When the one you tapped guesses the person in the circle you are describing, he chases him around the circle and tries to tag him before he can return to his place. Does everyone understand how to play the game?

CHILD: What happens if you get caught?

CHILD: Is the sheep it?

TEACHER: Yes, the sheep then becomes the farmer and the game is played again

(The children play the game and the teacher evaluates it with them.)

TEACHER: George, you seemed to be having a good time. What did you like about the game?

CHILD: I like to be chased, and I didn't get caught.

TEACHER: How can we help each other in this game?

CHILD: We have to listen when someone is talking?

TEACHER: We learned how to play a new game that was fun. What else did we learn?

CHILD: We learned that some of us look alike in some ways.

CHILD: And we learned that we are different in other ways.

CHILD: We used color words and we used the names of kinds of clothes that kids wear.

TEACHER: How were you able to tell who the sheep was?

CHILD: By listening to the person tell about him.

TEACHER: What did those of you who were farmers find that you had to do in telling about the sheep? What do you think, Jane?

CHILD: I had to be able to tell Mary exactly what George looked like. I had to explain it to her so she could tell the one I was talking about.

TEACHER: Fine! You seemed to have fun and also you saw the need for being able to talk well so that you could explain something to someone else.

WRITING EXPERIENCES
THROUGH PHYSICAL EDUCATION

It has been mentioned previously that writing is an expressive phase of language. Unlike the other language arts, writing involves a specific manipulative skill which is dependent to a certain extent upon a child's muscular development. For this reason it seems appropriate at the outset of this discussion to set forth the following guidelines in helping children with writing.

1. There are many different ways that a child holds a pencil. The general recommendation is that the child should hold it with the index finger and thumb, with the pencil resting on the middle finger and where the index finger and thumb meet. This position makes the pencil an extension of the forearm. If the child cannot hold the pencil in position, it may mean that he has not yet developed sufficient small muscle control. This control, which

begins in the larger back and shoulder muscles, can be improved by encouraging the child to do things to improve such development. Such popular child activities as swinging and climbing are important to such development.

2. Proper placement of writing paper is very important. The child can sit in a chair with his back straight. The next step is to have him interlock his fingers, folding his hands on the table in front of him. His joined hands form a triangle with the front part of his upper body. The paper is then placed under the writing hand. For right-handed children the head is turned slightly to the left, with the opposite position for left-handed children.

3. If the child is left-handed there might be a slight variation from the right-handed child in the use of paper and pencil. He may need to turn the paper slightly to the left, and he should hold the pencil in such a way that he can see what he is writing. It should be recognized that for a left-handed child, right to left is a more natural movement. He can be told that he always starts to write on the same side of the paper as that of his writing hand.

4. A child may have difficulty making strokes from top to bottom. If this is the case, it is helpful with some children to have them practice swinging their arms from front to back and from side to side. The purpose of this is to help the child develop a feeling of rhythmic movement.

5. Practically all children enjoy finger painting, and this experience can be helpful to the child in his beginning-to-write activities. With the finger painting process he can get the feel of letter formations by making circles, parts of circles, and lines. After this experience the same can be tried with a pencil.

6. With some children, when they are beginning to form letters, it is a good practice to associate the letter with something to arouse the child's interest. For example, an O is round like an orange, or an S is curled like a worm.

7. A practice that I call "talk writing" can be used with success. This involves having the child "say" the action as he forms a letter. For example, in forming an upper case L, you could have him say "down" as he makes the vertical stroke downward and "across" as he makes the horizontal stroke.

8. You can make part of a letter and then have the child complete it.

You also can have the child make a part of a letter and you can complete it.

Throughout the literature on the subject one finds emphasis placed upon the using of writing in daily living in relation to the real interests and concerns of children. More and more, educators are subscribing to the idea that the child's ability to express himself well in writing grows with the development of interests and the concerns which he is eager to express.

In view of the fact that modern procedures emphasize written expression as an integral part of the child's school experiences, it becomes essential that elementary schools provide opportunities for children to write in purposeful and meaningful situations. In that children like to write about things that are fun, one such opportunity might well be in the area of physical education because of the commanding interest that this area of the elementary school curriculum has for a majority of children. The following generalized list is suggestive of some of the possibilities for purposeful written expression arising out of elementary school physical education experiences.

1. There are some activities that actually require writing. For example, some of the blackboard games that are conducted in the classroom and referred to previously, provide fine opportunities for interesting written experiences.

2. Some teachers have found that it is very desirable and interesting practice to have children copy rules and regulations for various activities.

3. Children can be given the opportunity to engage in creative writing experiences by writing a story about a specific physical education experience and what it did for them.

4. Children may be asked to record certain physical education information in scrapbooks.

5. Another approach in writing about physical education experiences is to use the physical education reading content discussed in the previous chapter. In addition to having the children try to read a story after having engaged in the activity depicted in the story, they can be asked to copy the story as well.

I have conducted many experiments with the above procedures. It has been found that when children engage in this type of writing activity the formation of letters (legibility) is much better than when they are asked to form letters into words under other kinds of conditions.

Some other forms of "body use" in writing are found in (1) body letters, (2) big pencil, and (3) action word writing.

Body Letters

To form a letter it is important that the child develop a memory of the shape of the letter. Using the body or some of its parts to form letters can improve upon *visualization*. This involves *visual image* which is the mental reconstruction of a visual experience, or the result of mentally combining a number of visual experiences.

There are many ways that body letters can be formed. For example, the letter *c* can be formed with the child in a sitting position on the floor. He bends forward at the waist, bows his head, and stretches his arms forward. The letter *c* can also be formed with parts of the body. The index finger and thumb can be curled to make a *c*, or both arms can be used for a *c* by simply holding the arms to the side and bending them at the elbows.

The creative teacher in collaboration with the children will be able to work out numerous other body letter possibilities. It is a good practice to have both the child and the teacher form a body letter and then have the other guess what the letter is.

Big Pencil

When a child begins to form letters he should be provided the opportunity to do this in several ways. One way is for him to pretend that he is a *big pencil*. He becomes a big pencil by first standing with his hands joined in front of him. Next, he bends forward with his arms straight and his joined hands pointing toward the floor. The teacher calls out a letter and/or shows the child a large letter written in manuscript. The child goes through the movement of forming the letter by moving his joined hands as if he were a pencil.

Action Word Writing

For action word writing the teacher will need to prepare materials as follows. Cut heavy cardboard (white tagboard is preferred) into several pieces about six inches wide and twelve inches long. Such action words as *jump, hop,* and *run* are written in manuscript on one side of the card. The cards are placed in a pile at a given distance away from the child. At a signal he runs to the pile of cards. He selects one card, does what it says, and returns to his original position. For example, if it says "jump," he takes several jumps back to where he started. When he returns, he copies the word on a piece of paper and returns for another card. If desired, the activity can be timed to see how much the child improves each time the activity is played. Several children can participate at once in relay fashion.

Chapter 6

INTEGRATION OF
PHYSICAL EDUCATION AND MATHEMATICS

The areas recommended here for the integration of physical education and mathematics are: (1) number and numeration systems,
(2) arithmetical operations (addition, subtraction, multiplication, and
division), (3) geometries, and (4) mathematics physical education listening and reading content.

INTEGRATION OF PHYSICAL EDUCATION
AND NUMBER AND NUMERATION SYSTEMS

Opportunities for counting and using numbers abound in many
children's physical education experiences. For example, in tag games the
children who are caught can be counted and that number compared to
the number of children not caught. In activities requiring scoring there
are opportunities for counting and recording numbers. In fact, it is
difficult to identify any kind of physical education experience that does
not include the use of numbers.

In this section several physical education experiences are described.
For each activity the mathematical concepts involved are noted so that
teachers can more easily locate instructional activities for a given content
area. Furthermore, suggested applications for making the best use of
each activity are included. Some of the activities are especially useful for
introducing a mathematical concept. These involve the learner actively
and incorporate a dramatization of the concept physically. Others reinforce concepts and skills previously taught. These are activities that
provide needed practice in interesting and personally involving situations.
Of course, teachers will no doubt want to adapt many of the activities so
they can be used to develop mathematical concepts and skills other than
those cited in the descriptions.

Concepts: Rote counting, forward and backward; ordinal number ideas;
numeration

Activity: Pass Ball Relay

Children divide into teams. The team members form rows close enough so they can easily pass a ball overhead to the next child in the row. On a signal, a ball is passed over each child's head to the end of the row. As children pass the ball overhead, each child calls out the number of his or her position on the team (one, two, three, and so on) until the ball reaches the end of the row. When the last child on the team receives the ball, he calls his number and then passes the ball forward again. The next to the last child calls out his number, and the ball continues to be passed forward to the front of the team. The activity can be varied by passing the ball in different ways. For example, under the legs, or alternating over and under. The winner is the first team to pass the ball forward and backward with the correct counting both forward and backwards.

Application: Children gain skill in rote counting while engaged in this activity. Children *do* need to know the sequence of number names if they are going to be able to use that sequence for rational counting and in their study of arithmetic. The teacher may start the counting at any number, depending on the skills of the group. Teams of ten or fifteen children apply numeration concepts when the counting starts with numbers like 195 or 995.

Concept: Quantitative aspects of numbers and numeral recognition

Activity: I Want to Meet

Ten cards are prepared so that each of the numerals one through ten will appear on one card only. Distribute these cards, one to each child. Then give to each of the other children a number of objects (pegs, cards, paper clips), making sure that each of the quantities one through ten is represented at least once. The teacher calls out a number, as four, and asks the child who holds the card with the numeral on it to go to the front of the group and hold his card for all to see. The child then says, "I want to meet all fours." The children with four objects hold them up. Someone counts them, and those who hold the correct number of objects join the child who is holding the card with the numeral 4 on it. They then run to a goal at the opposite end of the activity area. The first child to reach the goal scores a point. The activity continues with other numbers called for. From time to time the teacher should change the objects and cards held by the children. The first child to score a specified number of points wins.

Application: This activity provides a personally involving and interesting situation to relate numerals with the quantitative aspect of numbers. Children can be helped to count out the number of objects they have.

Concepts: Rational counting; greater than; less than

Activity: Bee Sting

Three children are bees. They are in their hives marked on the activity area. The rest of the children are in the center of the area. The bees run out and try to catch (sting) the children. When a child is caught, he must go with the bee to the bee's hive. When all the children are caught, each bee counts those in his hive. Different children should have a chance to be bees.

Application: Children are provided an opportunity to practice rational counting. The relations greater than and less than are applied as the numbers of children in the hives are compared.

Concept: Rational counting

Activity: Chain Tag

A child is chosen as leader, and the leader chooses another child to assist him. The two join hands, and chase the other children attempting to tag one. When a child is tagged the chain grows, for he takes his place between the other two. The leader and his assistant, the first two children, remain at each end of the chain throughout the activity and are the only ones who are able to tag. Whenever the chain encircles a child, he may not go under the hands or break through the line. If the chain breaks, it must be reunited before tagging begins again. Every time another child is added to the chain, the leader counts out loud to determine how many children are in the chain. When the chain consists of five to ten children, the game ends. A new leader is chosen and the game continues in like manner.

Application: Children gain skill in rational counting as they determine the number of children in the chain. The sequence of number names becomes more automatic and the cardinal use of numbers is reinforced.

Concepts: Rational counting; reading numerals

Activity: Count and Go

The children line up along the long side of a rectangular hard surface activity area. There are parallel lines drawn in chalk on the activity area. These are unequal distances apart, and parallel to the long side of the activity area. The teacher stands across from the children with numeral cards. As the teacher holds up any card at random (numerals on the cards are from one to the number of chalk lines which are drawn), the children must count the lines as they run, skip, and the like toward the teacher. When the children have progressed as many lines as indicated by the numeral card, they stop and stand still. The child who reaches the far side first is the winner.

Application: Reading numerals and rational counting is reinforced as children move forward the varying number of lines indicated on the card. The activity can be varied by relating the directions to move to the operation of addition and subtraction, as is often done with a number line. Directions, such as *plus two* and *minus three,* could be presented, and the children would then proceed to carry out these directions in terms of moving forward or backward.

Concept: Quantitative aspects of numbers and counting
Activity: Ten Little Indians

The children form a circle, all facing in. Ten children are selected to be Indians, and each one is given a number from one to ten. As the tune is sung, the child whose number is called skips to the center of the circle. When the Ten Little Indians are in the center, the song is reversed. Again, each child leaves the center and returns to the circle as his number is called.

> One little, two little, three little Indians,
> Four little, five little, six little Indians,
> Seven little, eight little, nine little Indians,
> Ten little Indian boys.
> Ten little, nine little, eight little Indians, etc.
> One little Indian boy.

Application: Position and sequence of numbers is important in basic arithmetic concepts. In this rhythmic activity, children are helped to see the quantitative aspects of ordinal numbers. The subtraction concept may also be introduced through this activity.

Concept: Quantitative aspects of numbers and counting
Activity: Come with Me

The children stand close together in a circle. One child is *It. It* goes around the outside of the circle. *It* touches a child and says, "Come with me." That child follows *It. It* continues in the same manner, tapping children who then follow *It* as he goes around the outside of the circle. At any time *It* may call "Go home!" All the children following *It,* and *It* himself, runs to find a vacant place in the circle. The remaining child becomes *It* for the next time. At the beginning the teacher has the children count how many there are at the start.

It can count the children as he taps them. All the children also can be encouraged to count as *It* tags children. The number of children not tagged might also be counted.

Application: The children are able to practice counting varying size groups in this activity. By having *It* and all the children count as the children are tagged, each child is helped to see number names related to specific objects (in this case the objects are children).

Concepts: Greater than; less than; ordinal number ideas; even and odd numbers

Activity: Number Man

One child, the Number Man, faces the class which is standing on a line at the end of the activity area. Each child in the line is given a number by counting off—1, 2, 3, 4, etc. The Number Man calls out, "All numbers greater than _____." The children who have numbers greater than the one called must try to get to the other side of the activity area without being tagged by the Number Man. The Number Man may also call out, "All numbers less than _____." "All even numbers." "All odd numbers." Anyone who is tagged must help the Number Man tag the runners. Any child who runs out of turn is considered tagged.

Application: Children gain skill with number sequence while identifying numbers which are greater or less than a given number. When children are lined up in sequence, it can be observed that the sets of odd and even numbers involve every other whole number.

Concept: Counting—In multiples of ones, twos, fives

Activity: Count, Move and Stop

One child is *It.* He stands behind a finish line. All the other children are at a starting line that is drawn 25 to 50 feet away, parallel to the finish line. The children sit in a cross-legged position, arms crossed on chests, at the starting line. The child who is *It* hides his eyes and counts to ten (or 20 or 100, depending upon the skills of the group) in any way he chooses, by ones, twos, or fives. While *It* is counting, the players come to a standing position and move toward the finish line during the count. *It* must call the numbers loudly enough for all to hear. At the call of ten (or whatever number has been decided upon), *It* opens his eyes. All players must be seated cross-legged and with arms crossed on chest, at the point to which they have advanced. Any child caught out of position must return to the starting line and begin again. The activity continues in this manner until one child has crossed the finish line and is seated before *It* has completed the count. The first child over the line interrupts the count by calling "over." All children return to the starting line, and the activity begins again with this child as the new *It.*

Application: The activity provides the necessary repetition of counting by ones, twos, and fives for each child, since not only is *It* counting but each child is counting in order to determine his movement forward.

Concepts: Ordinal number ideas; multiples of three

Activity: Leader Ball

Two teams stand in circle formation. On a given signal the leader of each team passes a ball to the player on his right, who passes it to the next player, and so on until it reaches the leader. The leader calls, "first round" immediately and continues to pass the ball for the "second round" and "third round." At the end of the third round, the leader raises the ball to signify that his team has finished. A point is scored for the team finishing first.

Application: The time interval between "first round," "second round," and "third round" requires that children keep in mind which number comes next. A variation requires that after three rounds of play the ball is raised and a point is awarded, as above; however, the numbering of the rounds continues successively. During the second period of play, the leader counts "fourth round, fifth round, sixth round." Attention is drawn to numbers that are multiples of three

Concepts: Successive doubling; grouping pattern for Hindu-Arabic numeration (base two); powers of two

Activity: Muffin Man

Children stand in a circle. While all the children sing the question of the song "Muffin Man," two children stand still in the center of the circle where they place their hands on their hips and face each other. After the question is sung, the two children in the center clasp hands and skip around the inside of the circle as everyone sings the answer: "Two of us know the Muffin Man . . . " and so on. When they finish the answer, the two children stand in front of two new children. Everyone sings the question again, then the four children in the center clasp hands and skip around the inside of the circle as all the children sing the appropriate answer: "Four of us know the Muffin Man . . . " and so on. This procedure is repeated for eight, sixteen, and so on, depending on the size of the group.

Oh, do you know the Muffin Man,
the Muffin Man the Muffin Man?

Oh, do you know the Muffin Man
Who lives in Dury Lane?
Two of us know the Muffin Man,
the Muffin Man, the Muffin Man
Two of us know the Muffin Man
who lives in Drury Lane.

Application: Children gain experience with successive doubling through this rhythmic activity. The grouping pattern associated with base two numeration is also illustrated.

INTEGRATION OF PHYSICAL EDUCATION AND ARITHMETICAL OPERATIONS

Physical education activities can provide children with valuable experiences with the operations of arithmetic (addition, subtraction, multiplication, and division). The energetic involvement of children in such activities brings an interest and enthusiasm to the learning of arithmetic that many children need very much.

Activities described here incorporate the operations of arithmetic. Some activities involve the child with the meaning of the operation, and other activities include computing. For example, addition and subtraction are used in many activities that require scoring. For a given operation, activities focusing on the meaning of the operation should be incorporated into the instructional program before activities including computation.

In order to make it easier to find instructional activities for a given operation, the mathematical concepts involved in each are listed with the description of the activity. Also, each description is followed by a discussion designed to help teachers make the best possible application of the instructional activity. Teachers will want to be alert to opportunities to further extend the mathematical experiences of children with these activities by keeping records, charts, and graphs, and by developing concepts of average and percentage.

Teachers should feel free to adapt an activity, making it more appropriate for the developmental level of their students. Often, by merely substituting larger or smaller numbers, an activity can be made useful for a specific group of children.

Concept: Addition
Activity: Three Deep

The children stand by two's one behind the other, in a circle. All face the center. A runner and a chaser stand outside the circle. The chaser tries to tag the runner. In order to save himself, the runner may run around the circle and stand in front of one of the couples in the circle. This makes the group three deep, and the outside child in the group must now run. He is then chased and tries to save himself in the same way. The outside person in a group of three must always run. If the runner is tagged, he becomes the chaser and must turn and chase the new runner.

Application: The teacher assists the children in identifying groups of twos when the circle is formed in the activity. When a runner stands in front of a group of two, the teacher assists the children to identify that two and one make three. If the chaser has difficulty in tagging the runner, chaser and runner can be changed so that one child is not the chaser for too long a period of time.

Concept: Meaning of addition; number sentences; equals

Activity: Lions and Hunters

Two teams are established. One team, the hunters, begins by forming a large circle. The other team, the lions, is within the circle. The hunters use a large ball such as a beachball and attempt to hit as many lions as possible within a two-minute period. As the lions are hit, they go to the lion cage that has been marked in chalk on the activity area. When the teams change places, the second group of lions hit go to a second lion cage marked on the activity area. A scorer records the number of lions by each cage and completes the appropriate number sentence and labels as illustrated:

(cage)		(cage)		
3	+	4	=	7
addend	plus	addend	equals	sum

Note: In an activity of this nature children should be cautioned to hit below the waist with the ball.

Application: Involve all of the children in counting the lions in each cage and in counting the number of lions caught altogether. Emphasize the fact that "three plus four" tells how many lions were caught altogether, and "seven" also tells how many lions were caught. They are both names for the same number, and that is what "equals" means; it means "is the same as." Three plus four is the *same as seven*.

Concept: Addition; subtraction

Activity Add-A–Number Relay

The class is divided into several teams, and a number is recorded for each team on the chalkboard. (Use low, one-digit numbers at first.) The teacher writes or calls out a number, then the first member of each team runs to the board and adds this number to his team's number on the board. He returns to his team, and the next team member runs to the board and adds the same number to the new sum. Each child on the team does the same until the first team finished wins. Each team should start with different numbers to prevent copying. Size of numbers used will depend on the developmental level of the children.

Application: This activity provides reinforcement of addition facts and addition computation presented visually. Wide variation in the difficulty of the addition situation is possible by varying the numbers used. The same activity can be varied by using subtraction. When subtraction is the operation, be sure that the numbers recorded initially on the chalkboard are large enough to allow successive subtractions as indicated. The subtraction game is called "Subtract-A–Number Relay." In an activity of this nature a child can receive help from another child or the teacher if necessary. The purpose of this is to avoid embarrassment of some children.

Concepts: Basic addition facts; basic subtraction facts

Activity: Number Catch

Every child is given a number from one to ten. The teacher calls "Two plus two" or "Six plus one" and tosses a ball into the air. Any child whose number happens to be the sum of the numbers called can catch the ball. The other children run away as fast as they can until the child catches the ball and calls "Stop." At that time all the children must stop where they are and remain standing in place. The child with the ball may take three long, running strides in any direction toward the children. He then throws the ball, trying to hit one of the children. If he succeeds, the child who is hit has one point scored against him. The activity continues, with the teacher calling out another pair of addends. The children with the lowest number of points are the winners.

Application: This reinforcement activity encourages immediate recall rather than just figuring out the sum again. Assign the numbers nine through eighteen if the children have studied the basic addition facts with larger sums. If the activity is altered for the operation of subtraction, the teacher calls "eight minus three" and Six minus zero."

Concepts: One less than; meaning of subtraction

Activity: Ten Little Birds

After the children form a circle, ten children are selected for the birds, and they count off from one to ten. They go into into the center of the circle and stand in a line within the circle. When the verses are sung, the child in the center with the number being repeated "flies" back to his original position in the circle of children. This is repeated until all the birds have moved back with other children selected to be birds.

> Ten little birdies sitting in a line.
> One flew away and then there were nine.
> Nine little birdies sitting up straight.
> One fell down and then there were eight.
> Eight little birdies looking up to heaven,
> One flew away and then there were seven.
> Seven little birdies picking up sticks,
> One flew away and then there were six.
> Six little birdies sitting on a hive,
> One got stung and then there were five.
> Five little birdies peeking through the door,
> One went in and then there were four.
> Four little birdies sitting in a tree,
> One fell down and then there were three.
> Three little birdies looking straight at you.
> One flew away and then there were two.
> Two little birdies sitting in the sun,
> One went home and then there was one.
> One little birdie left all alone,
> He flew away and then there were none.

Application: This rhythmic activity provides children an opportunity to act out the concept of *one less than.* Stop the song at any point and have the children select the vertical and/or horizontal forms of the subtraction fact that records the action that has just taken place. Also, use the phrase *one less than* in the discussion. For example, after the third stanza a child chooses a card with the subtraction fact $8 - 1 = 7$ from a set of three cards. As the teacher points to the numerals he or she says, "Eight minus one equals seven. Seven is one less than eight."

Concepts: One less than; meaning of subtraction

Activity: Dodge Ball

The class is divided into two teams. One team forms a circle and the other team stands inside the circle. The regular game of Dodge Ball is played, with players comprising the circle trying to hit the team members in the center with a large rubber ball such as a beachball. The children in the center, to avoid being hit, may move about, jump, stoop, but they may not go outside the circle. When a child in the center is hit, he becomes a part of the circle. Each time a child is hit, the team forming a circle calls out the subtraction fact for the action which has just taken place. For example, if there are ten children in the center and one is hit, the children call out "Ten minus one equals nine," before throwing the ball again. The team with the largest number of children remaining in the center at the end of two minutes wins the game.

Application: This activity enables children to decide what subtraction facts describe the physical situation they are experiencing. As the number sentences in this activity are all presented orally, the teacher may want to follow with an activity involving the writing of number sentences both horizontally and vertically.

Concept: Subtraction

Activity: Animal Catch

Two parallel lines about 20 feet apart are marked off. One child, the Animal Catcher, stands in the center area between the two lines. On one of the lines the other children form in groups of four (or five, six, and so on) facing the Animal Catcher. Each group selects the name of an animal. The Animal Catcher calls the name of one group of animals. These children try to run to the opposite line without being tagged by the Animal Catcher. If so, they remain as animals. Those children who are caught help the Animal Catcher to tag members of the other animal groups when called.

Application: The teacher helps the children to identify groups of four or whatever size group is selected. At intervals during the activity the teacher has the opportunity to develop the meaning of subtraction by asking such questions as "How many horses were caught?" "How many did we start with?" and "How many horses are left?" Children can be helped to count out the answers if necessary.

Concept: Multiplication by two

Activity: Twice as Many

The children stand on a line near the end of the activity area and face the caller, who is standing at the finish line about 25 to 30 feet away. The caller gives directions such as "Take two hops. Now take twice as many. Take three small steps. Now take twice as many." Directions are varied in number and type of movement. Each direction is followed by "Now take twice as many." The first child to reach the finish line calls out, "Twice as many," and everyone runs back to the starting line. The caller tags all those he can before they reach the starting line. All those tagged help the caller the next time.

Application: Children are able to apply their knowledge of multiplication facts for the factor two in a highly motivating activity. The teacher may want to check each time a new direction is given to be sure the children have multiplied by two accurately and have the correct answer. Those children having difficulty could be helped to act out the multiplication fact called for.

Concepts: Multiples; multiplication facts

Activity: Back to Back

The children stand back to back with arms interlocked at the elbows. The teacher points to each group and, with the help of the children, counts by twos. If one child is left over the number one is added and the total number of children is thereby determined. The teacher calls for any size group, and on signal the children let go and regroup themselves in the size called for. If the teacher calls for a group of two, the children must find a new partner. Each time the children are regrouped, they count by twos, threes, or whatever is appropriate, and add the number of children left over. (If the resulting number is not the total number of children present, there has been an error and groups should be counted again.) Whenever the number called for is larger than the group already formed, the teacher may choose to ask how many children are needed for each group to become the size group that has just been called for. Whatever the size group is called for, the children must hook up back to back in groups of that number. A time limit may be set. The children who are left over may rejoin the group each time there is a call to regroup.

Application: This activity not only provides experience with the multiple of a given factor, but also informally prepares children for uneven division. In fact, they may want to predict the number of children who will be left over before the signal to start regrouping is given. If a chalkboard is available, the teacher may choose to write number sentences to record each regrouping. For example, if there are 25 children and groups of four have been called for, the record should show that six fours and one is 25 or $(6 \times 4) + 1 = 25$.

Concepts: Multiples of whole numbers; common multiples

Activity: Multiple Squat

Children stand in line or in a circle, and each is assigned a number in order, starting with one. The children say their numbers in turn. However, when their number is a multiple of three they squat but do not speak. A common variation requires that children also squat for any number for which the numeral has the digit of three in it. Multiples of different numbers can be used, of course. A more complex variation involves squatting for a multiple of either of two designated numbers; that is, three and four.

Application: Children develop skill in determining the set of multiples for a specified whole number. The activity can be adapted for more advanced children by having them squat only for common multiples of two numbers. For the numbers two and three they would squat for six, twelve, and so on. Children should be reassigned numbers frequently.

Concept: Meaning of division (measurement)

Activity: Triplet Tag

The children form groups of three, with hands joined. After the groups are formed, the teacher should write a division statement pointing out that the number of children in the class is the product, and the size of the groups is the known factor. To find the unknown factor the groups are counted. If one or two children are left over, that number is the remainder and it is also recorded. The groups stand scattered about the activity area. One group is *It* and carries a red cloth. The *It* group tries to tag another group of three. Hands must be joined at all times. When a group is tagged, it is given the red cloth, and the activity continues.

Application: In this activity, children act out the measurement meaning of division. By taking a moment to record the numbers in a division statement, children can relate the situation to the symbols they will use when working with paper and pencil.

Concepts: Meaning of division (measurement); effect of increasing or decreasing the divisor

Activity: Birds Fly South

Play begins with the entire class distributed randomly behind a starting line. The number of children in the class is the dividend (or product). A caller gives the signal to play by calling "Birds fly south in flocks of six" (or the largest divisor that will be used). The class runs to another line that has been designated as "South." At this point the children should be grouped in sixes. After observing the number of flocks (the quotient), the children who remain (that is, those who were not able to be included in one of the flocks) become hawks who take their places between the two lines. Then with the call "Scatter! The Hawks are coming!" the children run back to the other line, with the hawks attempting to tag them. Note is taken of who is tagged. Play continues, with the entire class taking its place behind the starting line. The caller then uses the next lower number for the call. If six was used first, five would be called next. "Birds fly south in flocks of five." This continues until groups of two have been formed and they return to the starting line. Each time the children should observe the number of flocks that are formed.

To score the activity, each child begins with a score which is the number called first. In the case illustrated above the number would be six. If a child is tagged, his score decreases by a point.

Application: At the end of the activity, consider the arithmetic which has been applied. If possible, record division number sentences showing the number of flocks formed when different divisors were used for the same dividend. Help the children form the generalization that, for a given dividend (product), when the divisor (known factor) decreases, the quotient (unknown factor) increases in value. After this pattern is established, the numbers called can be reversed beginning with the smallest divisor and working up to the highest divisor to be used. Here, the converse of the previous statement can be developed.

Concepts: Basic facts of arithmetic; greater than and less than; factors and multiples; common factors and greatest common factor; prime numbers

Activity: Catch the Thief

The class is divided into two teams of equal number, and members of each team are assigned a number, starting with one for each team. Teams line up 20 or 25 feet apart, and an object is placed at the center so that it is equidistant from the two teams. As children line up it is not necessary that they line up in ordinal sequence. Whenever the leader signals, the appropriate child or children from both sides run to the center and try to pick up the object and take it across their line before being tagged by a member of the other team. When successful, one point is scored for the team. The team with the highest score wins.

The choice of appropriate signals for play will depend upon previous experiences of the class. Suggestions include:

"Less than four"
"The sum of five and six"

"The difference between twelve and seven"
"Multiples of four"
"The product of three and five"
"Factors of 24"
"Common factors of eight and twelve"
"Greater than eight and less than twelve"
"Primes"
"The greatest common factor of 12 and 18"

Application: Children reinforce a number of skills, depending upon the choice of signals for play. A call such as "Multiples of zero" will help children generalize the zero property for multiplication as they observe that no children run forward. Also, attention can be directed to the fact that whenever factors for a given number are called for, children with the number one and the given number always get to run. The idea of the empty set is applied with a call like "Greater than five and less than three." To reinforce correct interpretation of similar symbolic (visual) expressions, an overhead projector can be used for presenting the signal.

Concept: Multiplication of fractions

Activity: Fraction Race

The class is divided into a number of teams. Members of each team take a sitting position, one behind the other a specified distance from a goal line. Starting with the first child on each team, each child is assigned a number (one, two, and so on). The teacher calls out a multiplication combination including a fraction and a whole number. The children whose number is the product stand, run to the goal line, and return to their original sitting position. If the teacher calls out "One-fourth times eight," all the number twos would run. Similarly, if the teacher calls out, "Two-thirds times twelve," all the number eights would run. The first child back scores five points for his team, the second child back scores three points, and the last child scores one point.

Application: This activity helps children to determine the product of a fraction and a whole number quickly and accurately. Adjust the difficulty of the examples to the experience of the children.

INTEGRATION OF
PHYSICAL EDUCATION AND GEOMETRIES

In this area there are activities using concepts from geometries of one, two, and three dimensions. As in the two previous sections of the chapter, for each activity described, the mathematical concepts and skills involved are listed, thereby aiding the teacher in finding activities which incorporate the content for which the children have the prerequisite background.

Following each description of an activity, suggested applications of the activity are discussed. For example, some activities can be used for initiating a concept and others help children visualize figures and relative values. There are activities during which children discuss and sharpen ideas. Other activities provide needed reinforcement for concepts and skills.

Many of these activities can be varied to incorporate concepts from other areas of mathematics. An excellent example of an activity which can be adapted for use with many mathematical topics is *Word Race*, described later. In fact, it is possible to vary activities sufficiently that physical education experiences can be included in the instructional program for almost every topic in mathematics.

Concept: One- and two-dimensional geometric figures

Activity: Show-A–Shape

Children are scattered about the activity area, far enough apart that each child has space for swinging arms and moving about. The leader calls "Take two turns and show a _____," specifying the two-dimensional geometric figure each child is to form with his arms or body. All children turn around twice, then form the figure named. For example, a circle can be suggested easily with both arms overhead as hands touch. By bending elbows but keeping hands and forearms rigid, different quadrilaterals can be formed. A child who touches his toes while keeping his legs straight makes a triangle. At times have children work in pairs to form figures.

Lines, line segments, rays, and angles can also be shown. Children can let their extended arms represent a part of a line, with a fist used to suggest an endpoint. An infinite extension can be suggested by pointing the finger. For angles, the torso can become the vertex as the arms are swung to different positions. Acute, right, and obtuse angles can all be pictured in this way. It could be a good idea for the teacher to go over some of these possibilities before the children engage in the activity.

Application: This activity helps children to learn that geometric figures are not just marks on paper, but that they consist of a set of locations in space. The activity can be used to introduce selected definitions, such as an obtuse angle. However, because many of the figures formed will be suggestive rather than precise, the activity will usually be used for reinforcement.

Concepts: Triangle; polygons

Activity: Triangle Run

A large triangle is marked off with a base at each vertex. Three teams of equal size are formed, and one team stands behind each base. On a signal the first child of each team leaves his base and runs to his right around the triangle, touching each base on the way. When he returns to his base, the next child on his team does the same. The runners may pass each other, but they must touch each base as they run. The first team back in its original place wins.

Application: This activity helps to demonstrate certain properties of a triangle, for example, the three angles. It is best to mark off different-shaped triangles from time to time so that the properties observed can be generalized to all triangles. Other polygons can be illustrated by forming more than three teams.

Concept: Radius of a circle

Activity: Jump the Shot

Eight to ten children make a circle, facing the center. One child stands in the center of the circle with a beanbag tied to the end of a rope. The center child swings the rope around in a large circle low to the surface area in order for the beanbag to pass under the feet of those in the circle. The children in the circle attempt to jump over the beanbag as it passes beneath their feet. When the beanbag touches a child it is a point against him. The child with the lowest score wins at the end of a period of one or two minutes long. The child in the center may then exchange places with a child in the circle.

Application: The activity can be used to help children visualize the radius of a circle. They should note that the rope, which represents the radius, is the same length from the center to any point along the circle.

Concept: A circle is a simple closed curve; the interior of a circle

Activity: Run Circle Run

The class forms a circle by holding hands and facing inward. Depending on the size of the group, children count off by twos or threes (for small groups) or fours, fives, or sixes (for large groups of around 30). The teacher calls one of the assigned numbers. All the children with that number start running around the circle in a specified direction. Each runner tries to tag one or more children running ahead of him. As a successful runner reaches his starting point without being tagged, he stops. Runners who are tagged go to the interior of the circle. Another number is called, and the same procedure is followed. This continues until all have been called. Then the circle is reformed and new numbers are assigned to the children.

As the number of children decreases, a smaller circle can be drawn on the surface area inside the large circle; the children must stay out of the smaller circle when running around to their places.

Application: Help the children notice that when they form a circle by holding hands, they make a continuous, simple, closed shape. As they play the game, they should observe what happens to the size within the circle, the interior of the circle.

Concept: Interior of a figure

Activity: Three Bounce Relay

Teams are formed and make rows behind a starting line. A small circle about one foot in diameter is drawn 15 feet in front of the starting line before each team. At a signal the first child on each team runs with a ball to the circle. At the circle he attempts to bounce the ball three times within the circle; that is, in the interior of the circle. If the ball at any time does not land on the interior, the child must start over from the starting line. When a child has bounced the ball three times within the circle, he returns to the starting line and touches the next child, who does the same thing. The first team finished wins.

Application: The word *interior* is stressed in explaining the activity. The children can thus learn the meaning of this term by practical use. However, so that children do not associate the term only with circular regions, other geometric shapes can be drawn from time to time.

Concept: Two-dimensional geometric figures

Activity: Geometric Figure Relay

Two lines are drawn about 30 feet apart on an activity area. The class is divided into two teams, with both teams standing behind one of the lines. The teacher calls out the name of a geometric figure, and the teams run across to the opposite line and form the figure with hands joined. The first team that forms the figure correctly wins a point. The teams then line up behind that line and, when the teacher calls out another figure, they run to the opposite line and again form the figure the teacher has called. The geometric figure can be those that the children have been working with, and may include circle, square, rectangle, triangle, pentagon, rhombus, equilateral triangle, and the like. By letting a raised hand represent an end point and an extended hand the place of an arrow to indicate continuation, two-dimensional figures other than polygons can be called. Possibilities include line, line segment, ray, and half-line.

Application: By acting out their shapes, children gain familiarity with a variety of geometric figures and their properties.

Concepts: Geometric figures; mathematical vocabulary (varied topics)

Activity: Word Race

Two teams are selected, and both line up along a base line. Identical sets of cards are prepared for each team, with each card showing a definition or phrase in bold letters. The cards are distributed to members of the two teams with one card (or possibly two) per child. The leader stands beside a box on the surface area about 25 feet from the base line. He has a set of word cards with letters large enough to be read by the children. When the leader holds up a word card, the child with each team with the matching definition or phrase card runs to place his card in the box. The first team placing the correct card in the box wins a point. In order to minimize confusion as to which card is placed in the box first, different colors can be used for the two sets of cards.

Application: Children have many opportunities to discuss the definitions of mathematical terms as this activity progresses, and they learn much from each other. In fact, questions or misunderstandings may come to light which the teacher will want to deal with at an appropriate moment. A few examples of words for word cards and of matching definitions or phrases are listed below, but teachers will be able to think of others which relate directly to mathematics which is the immediate focus of instruction in the classroom. Of course, it is necessary to use definitions appropriate to the child's level of development.

Leader's Word Card	*Matching Card for Team Member*
triangle	a polygon with three sides
rhombus	a polygon with four equal sides
interior	includes all points inside
radius	from the center to the circumference
addend	tells how many in one of two parts of a set
factor	the results of dividing a product by a factor
prime number	has exactly two different whole number factors

Concepts: Geometric figures; mathematical vocabulary (varied topics)
Activity: Have You Seen My Friend?

Each child is assigned a mathematical name, a term which has been used in class. For example, one child may be a triangle and another a cube. Children could also be assigned names like factor, zero, and centimeter. Names should be printed on cards and either pinned on each child or placed around the neck with a string.

Appropriately named, the children stand or sit in a circle. One child is *It,* and he walks around the outside of the circle. Eventually, *It* stops behind one of the players and asks him, "Have you seen my friend?" The child in the circle answers, "What is your friend like?" *It* describes the mathematical concept which is the name of one of the other children in the circle. He may say, "My friend is a polygon, and he has four sides." The child in the circle attempts to guess which other child is being described, and as soon as he guesses correctly, he chases that child around the outside of the circle. The child being chased tries to run around the circle and return to his place without being tagged by the chaser. If he is tagged, he becomes *It.* If he is not tagged by the chaser, the chaser becomes *It.* The child who was *It* before the chase merely steps into the place made vacant by the chaser.

Application: During this activity, discussion concerning correct and adequate definitions of mathematical concepts are likely to evolve. For example, if a child describes his friend as "a polygon with four sides" and one child is named "square" and another "rhombus," the fact that the description could have applied to either is likely to come to light. When selecting mathematical terms to use, needed reinforcement can be provided by focusing on ideas which have been studied recently.

Concepts: Parallel lines; right angles
Activity: Streets and Alleys

The children divide into three or more parallel lines with at least three feet between children in each direction. A runner and a chaser are chosen. The children all face the same direction and join hands with those on each side forming "streets" between the rows. Dropping hands, the children make a quarter turn and join hands again and form "alleys." The chaser tries to tag the runner going up and down the streets and alleys but not breaking through or going under arms. During the activity, the teacher aids the runner by calling "streets" or "alleys" at the proper time. At this command the children drop hands, turn and grasp hands in the other direction, thus blocking the passage for the chaser. When caught, the runner and chaser select two others to take their places.

Application: Children should be helped to notice that the lines of children represent parallel lines. Further, when the teacher calls "alleys" and the children make a quarter turn, children can associate the turn with a right angle.

Concepts: Circle; inside and outside; exploration of space

Activity: Inside Out

The class is divided into teams of four or more, and children on each team join hands to form a circle in which each child is facing toward the inside. When the leader calls, "inside out," each team tries to turn its circle inside out. That is, while continuing to hold hands the children move so as to face out instead of in. To do this, a child will have to lead his team under the joined hands of two team members. The first team to complete a circle with children facing toward the outside of the circle wins.

Application: This activity is designed as a kind of puzzle or problem-solving activity, for the goal is presented to the children and they are not told how it is possible to turn the circle inside out. It is designed to be the initial encounter with the process involved.

Concept: The shortest distance between two points is a straight line

Activity: Straight-Crooked Relay

The class is divided into four teams. In the relay have one team run directly between two points while the second team has an additional place to tag between the two points that is not in direct line with the other points. Teams should be switched so that they alternate, having to run the crooked route. Also, if desired the teams taking the crooked route can start with a little bit of a head start.

Application: The children can notice that it takes less time to move between two points by following a straight line than by a crooked line because it is the shortest distance. The children can measure the distance of the straight and crooked lines between the two points that are equidistant for the two teams. To account for individual differences of children, the teacher might make sure that both slow and fast runners are assigned to each team.

Concepts: The meaning of perimeter; the shortest distance between two points is a straight line.

Activity: Around the Horn

A small playing area is set up similar to a baseball diamond with a home plate and three bases. The team in the field has a catcher on homeplate and two fielders on each of the bases. The runners of the other team stand at homeplate. The catcher has the ball. The object of the activity is for the catcher and fielders, upon a signal, to relay the ball around the bases and back to homeplate *twice* before the runner at homeplate can run around and tag each base and proceed to homeplate *once.* At the bases, the fielders take turns. One takes the first throw, the other the second. The team up to the plate scores a point if it reaches homeplate before the ball.

Application: The distance around the bases is described at the perimeter of the field. Each runner is told he must run the perimeter of the field, and the team in the field is told that the ball must go twice around the perimeter of the field. The children learn that a wild throw which is not in a straight line to the other player takes longer to get to the next base.

MATHEMATICS PHYSICAL EDUCATION LISTENING AND READING CONTENT

Early attempts to develop mathematics physical education listening and reading content involved stories written around certain kinds of physical education experiences with the content also involving reference to mathematics experiences. These stories were used in a number of situations. It soon became apparent that with some children the internalization of the mathematics concept in a story was too difficult. The reason for this appeared to be that certain children could not handle both the task of reading while at the same time developing an understanding of the mathematics aspect of the story. It was then decided, as was suggested in Chapter 4, that since *listening* is a first step in learning to read, auditory input should be utilized. This process involved having children listen to a story, perform the activity, and simultaneously try to develop the mathematics concept. When it appeared desirable, this process was extended by having the children read the story after having engaged in the activity. The following is a description of one of the first experiments with a mathematics physical education story.

After the following story was written, it was used and evaluated by a first grade teacher with her class of 30 children. The name of the story is *Find a Friend* and it is an adaptation of a game called *Busy Bee.* The mathematics concepts inherent in the story are: *groups or sets of two, counting by twos,* and beginning *concept of multiplication.*

FIND A FRIEND

In this game each child finds a friend.
Stand beside your friend.
You and your friend make a group of two.
One child is *It.*
He does not stand beside a friend.
He calls, "Move!"
All friends find a new friend.
It tries to find a friend.
The child who does not find a friend is *It.*
Play the game.
Count the number of friends standing together.
Count by twos.
Say two, four, six.
Count all the groups this way.

The group of first grade children with which this experiment was conducted bordered on the remedial level and had no previous experience in counting by twos. Before the activity, each child was checked for the ability to count by twos and it was found that none had this ability. Also, the children had no previous classroom experience with beginning concepts of multiplication.

The story was read to the children and the directions were discussed. The game was demonstrated by the teacher and five pairs of children. As the game was being played, the activity was stopped momentarily and the child who was *It* at that moment was asked to count the groups by twos. The participants were then changed, the number participating changed, and the activity was repeated.

In evaluating the experiment it was found that this was a very successful experience from a learning standpoint. Before the activity none of the children were able to count by twos. A check following the activity showed that 18 of the 30 children who participated in the game were able to count rationally to ten by twos. Seven children were able to count rationally to six, and two were able to count to four. Three children showed no understanding of the concept. No attempt was made to check beyond ten because in playing the game the players were limited to numbers under ten.

There appeared to be a significant number of children who had profited from this experience in a very short period of time. The teacher maintained that in a more conventional teaching situation the introduction and development of this concept with children at this low level of ability would have taken a great deal more teaching time and the results probably would have been attained at a much slower rate. Several experiments similar to this one were conducted with much the same results.

Following are several mathematics physical education stories. Included are the mathematics concepts inherent in the stories along with some teaching suggestions for each story.

JUMP AWAY

All children like to jump.
Six children stand in a line.
One child jumps away.
Now there are five children.
Another jumps away.
Now there are four.
Another jumps away.
Now there are three.
Another jumps away.
Now there are two.
Another jumps away.
Now there is one.
He jumps away.
Now all have jumped away.
Do it again.

Concepts: Subtraction through six; taking away one; geometric figure (line)

Teaching Suggestions

1. Be sure the children stand in a line; that is, shoulder to shoulder. (Standing one behind the other is a *column* or *row.*)
2. The teacher can call attention to the children that they are standing in a line. A line could be drawn to help them understand the geometric figure.
3. The teacher can ask the child who jumps away to call out how many there are left as he jumps or after he jumps. If he does not know he can turn around and count the number.
4. The teacher may wish to put the take away facts through 6 on flash cards and use them in connection with the activity. This might be

used as an evaluative technique after the children engage in the activity.

HOP AND JUMP

Stand straight.
Now stand on one foot.
Hop on this foot.
Hop again.
Now stand on both feet.
Jump with both feet.
Jump four times.
Tell how many times you hopped.
Tell how many times you jumped.
Tell how many more times you jumped.
Tell how many fewer times you hopped.

Concepts: Addition; subtraction; rational counting; inequality of numbers (more than, less than)

Teaching Suggestions

1. Have the children count as they hop and jump.
2. The activity can be repeated a number of times using different combinations.
3. For children who have difficulty remembering how many more or how many fewer, one foot print can be drawn on a piece of cardboard to represent a hop and two foot prints can be drawn on a piece of cardboard to represent a jump. The children can be given the cardboard and they can trace the outline of their own feet. The teacher can collect some of the cardboards of the foot prints. She can put two "hop" cards or four "jump" cards together.

COME WITH ME

Children stand close together in a ring.
One child is *It.*
It goes around the ring.
It will tap a child.
It will say, "Come with me."
That child will follow *It.*
It will tap another child.
It will tap many children.

They will all follow *It.*
It will say, "Go home!"
All run to a place in the ring.
It will try to get a place.
One child does not get a place.
Now he is *It.*
Tell how many were tapped.
Tell how many were not tapped.
Play again.

Concepts: Rational counting; addition; subtraction
Teaching Suggestions

1. Be sure the children know how many there are at the start.
2. *It* can count the children as he taps them.
3. It may be necessary in some cases to have the children who are not tapped counted by *It* before he calls, "Go home!"
4. A variation could be for the teacher to put individual numbers on flash cards. She can hold one of these up to show either how many should be tapped or how many are to be left. In this way the teacher can control the activity in terms of the number combinations with which she might wish to work.

MRS. BROWN'S MOUSETRAP

Some of the children stand in a ring.
They hold hands.
They hold them high.
This will be a mouse trap.
The other children are mice.
They go in and out of the ring.
One child will be Mrs. Brown.
She will say, "Snap!"
Children drop hands.
The mouse trap closes.
Some mice will be caught.
Count them.
Tell how many.
Tell how many were not caught.
Play again.

Concepts: Rational counting; addition; subtraction

Teaching Suggestions

1. All of the children can count together the number caught.
2. All of the children can count together the number not caught.
3. If the teacher wishes she can have the children who are caught stand in a line facing those not caught. This way the children can easily see the difference.

RUN ACROSS

The children stand in line.
They stand beside each other.
One child is *It.*
He goes in front of the line.
He calls, "Run!"
The children run to the other end.
It tags as many as he can.
Tell how many were tagged.
Tell how many were left.
The children who were tagged help *It.*
Again *It* calls, "Run!"
More are tagged by *It* and his helpers.
Tell how many were tagged.
Tell how many were left.
Play until all but one is tagged.
He will be *It* for next time.

Concepts: Addition; subtraction; rational counting; geometric figure (line)

Teaching Suggestions

1. All of the children can count together the number tagged.
2. All of the children can count together the number left.
3. If the teacher wishes she can have the children who are tagged stand in line facing those who are left. This way the children can easily see the difference.
4. The teacher can call attention to the children that they are standing in a line. A line could be drawn to help them understand the geometric figure.

TAKE AWAY, TAKE AWAY

Children stand in a ring.
One child is *It.*
He moves around the ring.
All children sing this song.
Sing it like you would sing, "Twinkle Twinkle Little Star."

Take away, take away, take away one.
Come with me and have some fun.
Take away, take away, take away two.
Come with me, oh yes please do.
Take away, take away, take away three.
All please come and skip with me.

Now sing and dance.
This is what *It* does while all sing.
It takes away one child by tapping him.
He follows behind *It.*
Sing until *It* taps three children.
At the end of the song all three try to get back to their places.
It tries to get a place.
Tell how many are left each time *It* takes away one child.
Sing and dance again.

Concepts: Subtraction; groups or sets of two or three
Teaching Suggestions

1. Be sure the children know how many there are at the start.
2. If the teacher wishes, the activity can be stopped each time after they sing to make it easier to tell how many are left.
3. After two children have been taken away it can be shown that they are now a group. This can also be shown after three are taken.

Chapter 7

INTEGRATION OF
PHYSICAL EDUCATION AND SCIENCE

Although the primary purpose of this chapter is to deal with more or less specific ways to integrate physical education and science, some mention should be made about how this can occur generally. The following generalized list is submitted to give the reader an idea of some of the possible ways in which opportunities for science experiences might be utilized through various kinds of physical education activities.

1. The physical principle of equilibrium or state of balance is one that is involved in many physical education activities. This is particularly true of stunt activities in which balance is so important to proficient performance.

2. Motion is obviously the basis for almost all physical education activities. Consequently, there is opportunity to relate the laws of motion, at least in an elementary way, to physical education experiences of children.

3. Children may perhaps understand better the application of force when it is thought of in terms of hitting a ball with a bat or in tussling with an opponent in a combative stunt.

4. Friction may be better understood by the use of a rubber-soled shoe on a hard-surfaced playing area.

5. Throwing or batting a ball against the wind can show how air friction reduces the speed of flying objects.

6. Accompaniment for rhythmic activities, such as the drum, piano, and recordings, help children to learn that sounds differ from one another in pitch, volume, and quality.

7. The fact that force of gravitation tends to pull heavier-than-air objects earthward may be better understood when the child finds that he must aim above a target at certain distances.

8. Ball bouncing presents a desirable opportunity for a better understanding of air pressure.

9. Weather might be better understood on those days when it is too inclement to go outside to the activity area. In this same connection, weather and climate can be considered with regard to the various sport seasons, i.e., baseball in spring and summer and games that are suited to winter play and cold climates.

It should be understood that this is just a partial list of such possibilities and a person with just a little ingenuity could expand it to much greater length.

The remainder of the chapter will be concerned with the following areas and ways to integrate physical education and science: (1) universe and earth, (2) conditions of life, (3) chemical and physical changes, and (4) science physical education listening and reading content.

INTEGRATION OF PHYSICAL EDUCATION AND THE UNIVERSE AND EARTH

The following physical education experiences contain science concepts in the broad area of the *Universe and Earth.* Descriptions of the activities as well as an application are given for each activity.

Concept: Planet's orbit around the sun

Activity: Planet Ball

The children form a single circle and count off by twos. The number ones step forward, turn, and face the number twos. The larger circle should be about four feet outside the inner circle. Two children, designated as team captains, stand opposite each other in the circle. The teacher stands in the center of the circle and represents the sun. Each captain has a ball which his team identifies as a planet. On a signal from the teacher, each ball is passed counterclockwise to each team member until it travels all the way around the circle and back to the captain. Any child who is responsible for the ball striking the floor, either through a poor throw, or failure to catch the ball, has to recover the ball. As both circles pass the ball simultaneously, the time is kept and recorded. The group that passes the ball around their circle first wins or scores a point. Groups should exchange positions every several rounds.

Application: Prior to playing the game the children should notice that the balls being passed around are the planets and that they are revolving around the sun, represented by the teacher. They should be helped to identify the balls that are being passed counterclockwise because that is the direction the planets orbit the sun. In using this game to illustrate the orbits of planets, it should be stressed that the path or orbit of the ball should be unbroken or uninterrupted. It should also be noted that each completed orbit was done with different amounts of time for each circle, that the inner circle tended to take less time to pass the ball around the circle. Children can be encouraged to find out the difference in the orbits of the planets, as well as the varying lengths of time of these orbits.

Concept: Earth's orbit around the sun

Activity: Earth's Orbit Relay

The children are arranged in two circles, each circle facing in. A captain is elected for each team, and they stand ready with rubber playground balls in their hands. On a signal each captain starts his team's ball around by passing to the child on his right. Upon receiving the ball, each child spins around and passes the ball on to the next child on the right. As the ball makes a complete circuit back to the captain, he calls, "One." The second time around he calls, "Two." This procedure is repeated until the first team to pass the ball around the circle five times wins.

Application: In this activity the children need to be helped to see they are dramatizing the way the earth revolves around the sun. The entire circle becomes the complete orbit of the earth. The ball represents the earth, and as it is passed from one child to the other, they can see how the earth revolves around the sun. Also, since each child must spin around with the ball before passing it on, the concept of earth's rotation on its axis may be shown. The children must always turn and pass counter-clockwise, since that is the direction of the earth's orbit.

Concept: The turning of the earth on its axis causes day and night

Activity: Night and Day

The children stand in a circle holding hands. One child is in the center of the circle and represents the earth. As the children hold hands, they chant,

Illery, dillery, daxis
The world turns on its axis.
Isham, bisham bay,
It turns from night to day.

While the children are chanting, earth closes his eyes and turns slowly with one hand pointing towards the circle of children. As he rotates slowly with eyes closed (night), he continues to point with his hand. At the word *day* he stops and opens his eyes (day). Earth then runs after the child (to whom he is pointing at the word *day*) around the outside of the circle until he catches him. When the child is caught, he becomes the new earth. The original earth joins the circle, and the game continues. It might be advisable to use a blindfold that the child can slip off at the end of the verse.

Application: The child in the center became the rotating earth. When his eyes were closed, it became night, and when his eyes were open, it became day. The children might be encouraged to think of the child being pointed to as the sun, since it is day when the eyes are opened, and the sun causes day.

Concept: Eclipse of the moon

Activity: Eclipse Tag

The children are grouped by couples facing each other. The couples are scattered in any way about the play area. One child is chosen for the runner and is called Earth. Another child is the chaser. On a signal the chaser tries to tag Earth. Earth is safe from being tagged when he runs and steps between two children who make up a couple. When Earth steps between the two children, he calls out "Eclipse." The chaser must then chase the child in the couple toward whom Earth turns his back. If the chaser is able to tag Earth, they exchange places.

Application: The activity enables children to dramatize the concept of an eclipse of the moon so that they can see what occurs. The children should be helped to identify that when Earth steps between two children, the one he faces is the moon and his back is turned to the sun, and the earth's shadow covers the moon.

Concept: Force of gravity

Activity: Spoon Ball Carry

The children are divided into several teams. The teams stand in rows behind a starting line. A large spoon holding a tennis ball is given to the first member of each team. On a given signal they run with the spoons and balls to a designated point and back. They then hand the spoons and balls to the next team members. The team finishing first wins. If a ball drops from a spoon, it must be scooped up with the spoon and not touched otherwise. Some variety can be created by using balls of different sizes and weights. These various sized balls can be used at set intervals during one relay or in separate relay races.

Application: The concept of gravity is inherent in this activity. The children's attention should be directed as to why the ball seldom drops from the spoon and why, when it does, it falls down, not up. The use of a variety of sizes and weights of balls may create curiosity on the part of the children. Children can be helped to notice that they have more success in carrying a larger and heavier ball than one which is small and lighter. This experience can be directed toward further research by the children on questions posed by the group.

Concept: Force of gravity

Activity: Jump the Shot (This activity was described in Chapter 6 but is described again here for purposes of continuity.)

The children form a circle with one child in the center. The center child has a length of rope with a beanbag attached to one end. He holds the rope at the other end and swings the rope around close to the ground. The children in the circle must jump over the rope to keep from being hit. Any child who fails to jump and is hit receives a point against him. The child with the least number of points at the end of the game is the winner.

Application: The activity is played in small groups, and each child should have a turn to be in the center and swing the rope. The teacher might ask the children what they felt on the other end of the rope as they swung it around; that is, if they felt a pull. The teacher can ask what would happen if the rope broke or they let go of their end. This can be demonstrated. Further questions can lead to what kept the rope and beanbag from flying off during the game, that an inward pull on the rope kept the beanbag moving in a circular pattern, The teacher might also relate this to the manner in which planets travel in a circular orbit around the sun, and the moon around the earth, because of gravitational force.

Concept: Gravitational pull—of tides, planets

Activity: Planet Pull (Tide Pull)

The children are divided into two teams. One can be named Earth and the other Moon. The first child on each team kneels down on all fours, facing a member of the other team. There is a line drawn on the surface area between them. Each child has a collar made of a towel or piece of strong cloth placed around his neck. Each child grabs both ends of the other person's collar. The object is for each one to try to pull the other one across the line. The child who succeeds scores a point for his team. Each child on the team does the same. The team with the most points wins.

Application: This activity can be used to demonstrate the gravitational pull of earth and the moon, or the planets and the sun. It might be pointed out that a large child often was stronger and was usually able to pull a smaller child across the line, just as with members of the solar system being pulled to the largest member, the sun. Children should be cautioned to pull straight forward and not to either side. This is to avoid possible injury.

Concept: Earth's atmosphere—wind is moving air

Activity: Hurricane

The children are divided into two teams. Each team lines up on either side of a small playing area with lines drawn six feet apart on each side. In the center is a small, light object such as a ping-pong ball. Each child has a fan made of newspaper, cardboard, or some other type of suitable material. On a given signal the children fan the ball toward the opposite goal line. Each time the ball goes over the goal, a point is scored. The team having five points wins the game.

Application: In this activity the children can see that their fans create a wind. The wind is moving and makes the ball move. Children might experiment with different types of fans and ways of fanning to see if they can create stronger air movements.

Concept: Earth's atmosphere—force or lift of air

Activity: Air Lift

The children are divided into teams of four to six members each. One team stands on one side of a net stretched across the center of the court. (The size of the court may vary.) The game is started by one child throwing a rubber ring over the net. Any opposing team member may catch the ring and throw it back. The ring may not be relayed to another child on the same team. Play continues until a point is scored. A point is scored each time the ring hits the ground in the opponents' court or when any of the following fouls are committed.

1. Hitting the net with the ring.
2. Throwing the ring under the net.
3. Relaying the ring or having two teammates touch it in succession.
4. Throwing the ring out of bounds if opposing team does touch it.

The team scored upon puts the ring in play again. Five to fifteen points is a game, depending on the skill of the group.

Application: The ring is used to represent an airplane, and the children's attempts to toss it over the net without allowing it to fall can be compared to *lift*. In attempting to toss the ring over the net, many fouls may be committed, and it should be pointed out that this is due to both the insufficient amount of force of air, the downward pull of gravity, and also poor aiming. In most cases more force or lift is needed to launch a ring, or plane. When each point is made, it can be referred to as a plane successfully launched. The children might be encouraged to find out how planes are launched from aircraft carriers. They may conclude that a plane must have an enormous lift before it can rise. It can be further pointed out that the force that produces the lift to cause a plane to rise is caused by movements of air and that this movement produces low pressures over the top of the wings and high pressures under the bottom of the wings.

Concept: Earth's atmosphere—water cycle

Activity: Water Cycle Relay

The children are divided into teams of six children each. Each child is assigned a part of the water cycle in the order of the process, for example, (a) water vapor, (b) rain, (c) land, (d) stream, (e) river, and (f) ocean. The teams are seated in rows close enough to be able to pass a ball from one child to the next. On a signal the first child of each team calls his part of the water cycle (water vapor), passes the ball to the second child on his team, and runs to the end of his team's line. The second child calls out his part (rain), passes the ball to the next team member, and moves back in the same manner. This procedure continues until each team has made three complete cycles. The first team to finish wins.

Application: The cycle is represented by the children moving in turn. As the children pass the ball, it should be emphasized that the various stages are represented by each child. It is important that the children notice the correct order within the cycle and situate themselves in the line accordingly. The ball represents water regardless of the form it takes within the cycle. The activity may be adapted by changing the rain part of the cycle to snow or sleet and by adding brooks and bays if the children so choose.

INTEGRATION OF PHYSICAL EDUCATION AND CONDITIONS OF LIFE

Concept: Variety of life—animals live in many kinds of homes

Activity: Squirrels in Trees

With the exception of one child, the children are arranged in groups of three around the activity area. Two of the children in each group face each other and hold hands, forming a hollow tree. The third child is a squirrel and stands between the other two children. The extra child, who is also a squirrel stands near the center of the activity area. If there is another extra child, there can be two squirrels. The teacher calls, "Squirrel in the tree, listen to me; find yourself another tree." On the last word *tree*, all squirrels must run and get into a different hollow tree, and the extra squirrel also tries to find a tree. There is always one extra squirrel who does not have a tree. At different points in the game, the teacher should have the children change places. The game can be adapted for other animals such as beavers in dams, foxes or rabbits in holes, bears in caves, and the like.

Application: In playing this game, children can name other animals and the kinds of homes in which they live. They can be encouraged to figure out how they could dramatize the different types of homes animals have such as the two children forming the hollow tree.

Concept: Variety of life—animals move about in different ways

Activity: Animal Relay

The children divide into several teams. The teams stand in rows behind a line about 20 feet from a goal line. The object of the relay is for each team member to move forward to the goal line and return to his place at the rear of his team, moving as quickly as he can according to the type of animal movement assigned. Relays may be varied by the children going to the goal line and back doing the following imitations of various animals.

Donkey Walk—traveling on all fours, imitating a donkey's kick and bray.

Crab Walk—walking on all fours, face up.

Bear Walk—Walking on all fours, feet goint outside of hands.

Rabbit Hop—child moves forward, bringing his feet forward between his hands.

On a signal the teams proceed with the relay, using the movements indicated by the teacher. The first team finished wins.

Application: By dramatizing the various movements of animals, children are helped to learn about the differences among animals. Children can be encouraged to figure out ways of moving to represent many types of animals.

Concept: Interdependence of life

Activity: Fox and Geese

The lines are drawn on opposite ends of the activity area. One child is the fox and stands in the center of the area. The other children are the geese and stand behind one of the end lines. When the geese are ready, the fox calls "Run!" and the geese must then run and attempt to cross the opposite end line before the fox can catch them. The geese are not safe until they have crossed this line. The children who are tagged by the fox must help the fox tag the remaining geese the next time. The geese who have not been tagged line up at the end line and, on a signal from the fox, run back to the original starting line. When the geese have run three times, a new fox is chosen.

Application: Through this game the children learn that animals eat other animals as a means of survival and that these types of animals are called carnivorous. The children might find out various animals that are natural enemies and substitute their names for fox and geese.

Concept: Interdependence of life

Activity: Spider and Flies

Two goal lines are drawn at opposite ends of the activity area and a circle equal distance between the two goal lines. The children stand around the edge of the circle, facing the center. One child, the spider, sits in the center of the circle. The other children are flies. The spider sits very still while the other children (the flies) walk or skip around the circle, clapping their hands as they go. At any time the spider may suddenly jump up and chase the flies. When he does, the flies run toward either goal. A fly tagged before reaching one of the goal lines becomes a spider and joins the first spider in the circle. The original spider always gives the starting signal to chase the flies, and other spiders may not leave the circle to chase the flies until he gives this signal. The last child caught becomes the next spider.

Application: The children should be encouraged to cultivate their quickness. The spider should be urged to jump up suddenly in order to surprise the flies. In this game the children can be helped to understand the interdependence of animals for food by the dramatizing of animals hunting each other for food and the victims seeking shelter for protection.

Concept: Interdependence of life—animals have to protect themselves
        from one another

Activity: Fox and Sheep

One child is selected to be the fox and stands in his den, a place marked off on one side of the activity area. The rest of the children are the sheep. They stand in the sheepfold, another area marked on the opposite side of the activity area. The remaining part of the area is called the meadow. The fox leaves his den and wanders around the meadow, whereupon the sheep sally forth and approaching the fox, ask him, "Are you hungry, Mr. Fox?" Should the fox say, "No I am not," the sheep are safe. When the fox says, "Yes I am!" the sheep must run for the sheepfold, as the fox may then begin to chase them. The fox tags as many sheep as he can before they find shelter in the fold. Those sheep who are caught must go to the fox's den and thereafter assist the fox in capturing sheep. The original fox is always the first one to leave the den. He also is the fox who answers the sheep's questions. The last sheep caught becomes the fox for the next game. The game can be adapted by using other animals who are natural enemies to each other as cat and mouse, hound and rabbit, or fox and geese.

Application: The same application can be used as for Spider and Flies.

Concept: Interdependence of life—conservation of forests

Activity: Forest Lookout

The children form a circle and count off by twos. All of the ones form a circle; all of the twos form a second circle so that there is a double circle with all the children facing inward. The children on the inside circle represent trees. Each member of the outside circle represents a fire fighter and stands behind one of the trees. One child is the Lookout; he stands in the center of the group. The lookout calls loudly, "Fire in the forest! Run, run, run!" while clapping his hands. All the fire fighters in the outside circle begin running to the left. While the fire fighters are running, the lookout quietly takes a place in front of one of the trees. The runners who observe the lookout doing this, do likewise. The fire fighter left without a tree becomes the lookout for the next game, and the trees become the fire fighters for the next game.

Application: This activity helps to emphasize the importance of protecting the forests from fire. It can be brought out that many animals lose their homes if the trees burn and that small plants are also destroyed.

INTEGRATION OF PHYSICAL EDUCATION
AND CHEMICAL AND PHYSICAL CHANGES

Concept: Molecular structure of water (H_2O)

Activity: Water-Water

The children form a circle holding hands and one member is *It* and stands in the center of the circle. (*It* represents oxygen.) *It* tries to break out of the circle between the children by trying to make them break their grip. If *It* succeeds in breaking through the circle, he immediately runs in either direction around the circle pursued by both of the members who broke the chain. If *It* is tagged by either of the other two members before he can return to one of their places in the circle, he has to try to break out of the circle again or another child can be selected to be *It.* If *It* eludes the chasers and returns to the circle before being tagged, the last chaser returns to the circle and can become *It.*

Application: The simple structure of water can be used as an introduction to molecular structure of matter. Discussion can relate this game to the structure of water, that is hydrogen (two parts) oxygen (one part). With the circle representing a molecule of water and *It* representing one part of oxygen, and the two chasers representing two parts of hydrogen, the children can get a feel for a better understanding of molecular structure of other elements of matter.

Concept: Movement of molecules in solids, liquids, and gases
Activity: Molecule Ball

The children arrange themselves in a circle. The group then counts off by twos. The number ones face inward, and the number twos face outward; that is ones and twos are facing each other. Each captain has a ball that is to be moved around the circle until it travels back to the captain. The exact manner in which the balls are to be moved around the circles is determined by the leader calling, "solid," "liquid," or "gas." When "gas" is called, the ball is to be thrown from one child to the next; when "liquid" is called, the ball is to bounced from one child to the next, and when "solid" is called, the ball is to be passed to the next child. When the ball completes the circle, the team which does so first is the winner. Whenever a child drops or does not catch the ball passed to him, he must retrieve the ball, return to his place in the circle, and then continue to move the ball to the next child.

Application: The use of *solid, liquid,* and *gas* as call words to change the speed of the balls' progress around the circles emphasizes the difference in speed of molecule's movement in solids, liquids and gases. The children can be helped to notice that the method of moving the ball around the circle relates to the speed of the movement of molecules in these different states of matter.

Concept: Molecules are in rapid and ceaseless motion
Activity: Molecule Pass

The class is divided into four groups, with each group standing in a straight line. The four groups form a rectangle with each group representing one side of the rectangle. The captain of each group stands near the center of the rectangle in front of his group. On a signal each captain throws his ball to his group, starting at the right. As each child receives the ball, he throws it back to his captain and assumes a squatting position. When the captain throws the ball to the last child in his group, he runs to the right of his group as the rest of the children stand. The last child on the left runs with the ball to the captain's place, and the procedure is repeated.

Application: Each ball represents a molecule of matter. The balls are kept in motion at all times. The children can be helped to notice that the ball (the molecule of matter) has to be kept moving. This can lead to a discussion of molecules of different substances: the greater space and rapid movement of molecules of gases (depending on area temperature), the less space and less rapid movement of molecules of liquids, and the lesser space and least rapid movement of molecules of solids.

Concept: Chain reaction comes from one molecule hitting another (or neutrons in radio active materials)

Activity: Tag and Stoop

The children are scattered over the activity area. One child is *It* and tries to tag two children, one with each hand. When *It* tags the first child, he then grasps the hand of that child. The two continue running after other children until *It* is able to tag a second child. *It* then stands still and gets down in a stooping position. The two children tagged now each try to tag two others and then they stoop down. The four children tagged now continue in the same manner. The object of the game is to see how long it takes for everyone to be tagged.

Application: In trying to demonstrate chain reaction, the increasingly powerful effect of a small beginning should be brought out. As the children watch the spread of those who are being tagged, they can see this effect.

Concept: Burning is oxidation: the chemical union of a fuel with oxygen

Activity: Oxygen and Fuel

One child is chosen to be fuel and another child is oxygen. The remaining children join hands and form a circle, with fuel in the center of the circle and oxygen on the outside of the circle. The children in the circle try to keep oxygen from getting into the circle and catching fuel. If oxygen gets in the circle, the children in the circle then let fuel out of the circle and try to keep oxygen in, but they must keep their hands joined at all times. When oxygen catches fuel, the game is over, and they join the circle while two other children become fuel and oxygen. If fuel is not caught in a specified period of time, a new oxygen can be selected.

Application: One child represents the fuel (as trees in a forest) and another the oxygen (the air). The children in the circle are the pre- venters of fire. If oxygen catches fuel and ignites him by tagging him, a fire is started. Then the game is over. In this manner children can be helped to see that oxygen feeds fire and that oxygen must be kept from fires that have started in order to put them out. The children might be encouraged to find out ways that fires are smothered, depending upon the type of burning material.

Concept: When light strikes a solid object, it bounces

Activity: Light Bounce

The children are divided into several teams. Two lines are marked on the surface area, parallel to a blank wall. One line is drawn six inches from the wall and is the goal line. The second line is drawn 12 feet from the wall. Behind this second line, the teams stand in rows. Each team is given a small wooden block. The first child on each team takes a turn throwing his block. If the block lands between the goal line and the wall, a point is scored for that team. If the block falls outside the goal line, each other team gets one point. Each child on the teams proceeds in the same manner until each child has thrown. The team with the highest score wins.

Application: Children can be helped to notice that the wooden blocks rebound from the wall just as light rays do upon coming in contact with a solid object.

Concept: Heat and light can be reflected

Activity: Heat and Light

The children are divided into several teams. The teams make rows at a specified distance from the blank wall of a building. The first child on each team throws a ball against the building and catches it as it bounces back to him, passes it over his head to the next child on the team, and then moves to the end of the line. The team to complete the procedure first wins.

Application: Attention can be called to the fact that just as the ball hits the wall and bounces back, so light and heat are reflected; that is, light and heat are reflected (or bounded off) by a mirror or other shiny surface.

Concept: A prism can separate a beam of white light into a spectrum

Activity: Spectrum Relay

The class is divided into two teams so that there will be seven children on each team. Each child forms a row behind a starting line. Then the children on each team are assigned a specific color of the spectrum and stand in the correct order that colors appear in the spectrum; that is, red, orange, yellow, green, blue, indigo, and violet. Each child is given the appropriate color tag to pin on his clothing so that his teammates can quickly see where to line up. Those children who are not assigned a relay team are the prism and stand at a given distance away from the starting line and space themselves several feet apart, facing the relay teams. On a signal all the children on each team must run between and around back of the children standing a distance away (the prism) and return to the starting line. The team members must then join hands so that each team finishes by being lined up on correct order of colors in the spectrum behind the starting line. The first team lined up correctly behind the starting line wins. A few children may change places with those who did not have a chance to run in the first relay.

Application: This relay provides children with the opportunity to dramatize the concept of the prism. The teams represent the beams of light before passing through the glass prism (represented by the children standing a distance away) and that after they passed through the glass prism, they then represented the band of colors called the visible spectrum. During the discussion it can be pointed out that each color of light travels through the glass prism at a different speed. The children can be encouraged to find about different things in nature that serve as prisms to create visible spectrums.

Concept: Heavy load can be moved more easily by use of machines

Activity: Wheelbarrow

This is a couple stunt and each child has a partner of about equal size and strength. One child assumes a position with his hands on the surface area, with his arms straight and his feet extended behind him. The other child picks up the feet of the first child who keeps his knees straight. The first child becomes a wheelbarrow by walking along on his hands while the other child holds on to his legs. The children change positions so that each can become a wheelbarrow. Couples can perform separately or teams can be formed to run a wheelbarrow relay.

Application: This activity can help the children understand how machines can make work easier. The child acting as the wheelbarrow will see that he is doing more work while the child operating the wheelbarrow uses very little effort.

Concept: Energy is needed to stop rapidly moving objects (Newton's law of inertia)

Activity: Jump the Brook Relay

The children are divided into teams. The teams stand in rows behind the starting line. The goal line is a good running distance away. Two lines, approximately three feet apart, are drawn parallel about 10 feet from the goal line. The space between the two center lines represents the brook. On a signal the captain of each team runs to the brook, stops, jumps over the brook with two feet together, runs to the finish line, and then returns to the starting line in the same way. He touches the second child on his team and then goes to the rear of his team. This procedure is continued until all the team members have jumped the brook. The team finishing first wins. Any child who fails to jump the brook (and so falls in) must return to the starting line and begin his turn again. The teacher may therefore adjust the size of the brook according to the limitations of the group.

Application: Children can discover that it takes great effort on their part to stop themselves when they reach the brook in order to make their jump with two feet together. When they stop suddenly, they find that while they might be able to stop their feet, the upper part of their bodies continues to move forward. Actually trying to stop on their part involves body energy or force. The children can also be encouraged to experiment and find that the faster they run, the more energy they have to expend to stop themselves.

Concept: Principle of inertia

Activity: Tug of War

The class is divided into two teams. A line is drawn between the teams as a goal line. The teams line up on each side of the goal line. Each member grabs hold of the rope in a single file fashion at the same distance from the goal line. Both teams are now in position to pull against each other. On a signal they begin pulling. The team that pulls the other over the goal line first wins the game.

Application: If each team in the Tug of War pulls just as hard as the other, there is no motion in either direction. If one team is stronger than the other, then there will be an unbalanced force, causing the other team to be pulled over the goal line in the direction of the stronger team.

Concept: A body left to itself, free from the actions of other bodies, will, if at rest, remain at rest

Activity: Pin Guard

The children form a circle. Ten pins or other suitable objects are set up in the middle of the circle. One child is selected as a guard to protect the pins. On a signal the children start rolling a ball to knock over the pins. The guard tries to keep the ball away from the pins by kicking it back toward the circle. The child who succeeds in knocking down a pin becomes the new guard.

Application: The pins in this game represent the body at rest (inertia) and the ball the force that puts the body in motion. It can be pointed out to the children that the pins in the center of the circle remain at rest until an outside force (the ball) strikes the pins and puts them in motion.

Concept: Laws of motion (acceleration is in proportion to the force that caused it and in the same direction as that force)

Activity: Balloon Ball

The class is divided into two teams. Each team divides into three groups. If a classroom is used, rows one, three, and five are team A. Rows two, four, and six are team B. The space on the outside of the first and sixth rows are the goals. If the game is played outside, the teams may sit in the same manner with lines drawn outside the first and sixth rows to serve as goal lines. A balloon is tossed into the air in the center of the room by the teacher. The seated children strike the balloon with the open hand and try to get it over their opponents' goal. The children may not strike the balloon with their fist or leave their seats. If either of these violations is committed, the balloon is tossed into the air by the member of the team that committed the violation. Each goal counts one point. The team scoring the greater number of points wins the game. If too many goals are made, one child from each team may be chosen to be goalkeeper. They may stand and try to prevent the balloon from striking the floor in their respective goal areas.

Application: It can be pointed out to the children that when they hit the balloon, it moves in the same direction as their hand. They also can be helped to notice that if the balloon is tapped lightly, it moves a short distance, and if it is hit hard it moves a longer distance. The activity dramatizes the concepts involved in Newton's laws of motion in a way children can see and understand.

Concept: Friction

Activity: Siamese Twins

The children get in pairs and sit back to back with arms folded and legs extended straight ahead and together. The object is to see which pair can stand first with feet together while maintaining the folded arm position.

Application: Before the game children can talk about some of the results of friction, such as heat and the resulting problems confronting scientists who design space missiles. The class might discuss ways in which friction helps us; that is the friction between the feet and ground when we walk and how we use snow tires or chains to provide friction in snow and icy weather. During and after the game the teacher can help the children see how the friction of their feet against the floor keeps them from sliding down. After the game the children might plan to chart lists of ways in which friction helps us.

Concept: Friction

Activity: Shoe Box Relay

The class is divided into several teams. The teams stand in rows behind a starting line 20 to 30 feet away from the goal line. Each team is given two large shoe boxes. The first child places his feet in the shoe boxes and advances to the goal line by sliding his feet along in a walking motion. When he crosses the goal line, he then returns to the starting line. The second child then places his feet in the shoe boxes and proceeds in the same manner. The first team to complete the race with all the team members in line behind the starting line wins. It is a good idea to have extra shoe boxes in case one becomes mutilated.

Application: From this activity the children can be shown that friction occurs whenever two surfaces rub together, and the larger the two areas moving against each other, the greater the friction. The children might discuss how tired their legs get and how much more difficult this means of locomotion is than walking.

Concept: Machines make work easier—arm as lever

Activity: Hot Potato

The class is divided into even number lines of five or six children each, separated at arms length from each other. Each line faces another line five to twenty feet away. Each child has a turn holding a ball at chest height in one hand and hitting it with the palm of the other hand, directing the ball to the line facing him. Each child of the opposite line scores one point for each ball he catches. The child who catches the ball then proceeds to hit the ball back to the opposite line, and a child tries to catch the ball to score a point. The child with the highest score wins.

Application: The use of the arm as a lever can be demonstrated in this activity. The teacher might draw a picture on the board to show children how the arm works as a lever.

Concept: The lever (in the third-class lever the effort is placed between the load and the fulcrum)

Activity: Net Ball (Note: Two concepts can be developed by Net Ball)

Before the activity the children can be told that serving is a basic skill used in the game of net ball and that for a successful game of net ball, it is necessary to learn to serve the ball properly. The server stands on the end line facing the net. He holds the ball in his left hand about waist height in front of him and to the right. He hits the ball underhand with his right hand (heel of hand). The weight of his body is transferred forward to the left foot as the right arm moves forward in a follow-through movement. (This procedure is just the opposite for the left-handed child.)

The children are divided into two groups, each group spaced in a pattern on one side of the net facing the other group. Each child is given the opportunity to serve two or three times. Following practice, the game is started by one child serving the ball over the net. (The height of the net will depend upon the ability level of the children—it can be from three to eight feet.) Any opposing team member may hit the ball over the net. The ball may not be relayed to another child (as in volleyball) on the same team. Play continues until a point is scored. A point is scored each time the ball hits the surface area in the opponents' court or any of the following fouls are committed.

1. Hitting the net with the ball.
2. Hitting the ball under the net.
3. Relaying the ball or having two teammates touch it in succession.
4. Hitting the ball out of bounds if opposing team does not touch it.

Application: (The lever) During the practice it can be shown how the arm has acted as a lever in the serving action, that the elbow joint was the fulcrum, the forearm the effort, and the ball was the load. Children can then be encouraged to find other examples that would illustrate this type of lever; that is, a man swinging a golf club or a boy or girl swinging at a ball with a bat.

Application: (Force and acceleration) It can be noticed that the servers have difficulty getting the ball in the opposite court, that the ball either fails to go over the net or it is hit out of bounds on the opposite side. The teacher can stop the activity to ask what makes the ball go out of bounds. The children might notice that it was hit too hard. If the ball fails to go over the net, it can be pointed out that it was not hit hard enough. The teacher can then ask the class to explain what factor influences the speed and distance the ball travels (the force of the serve or how hard the ball is hit that governs the acceleration of the ball). The children can be encouraged to apply this concept to other types of activities such as batting a baseball, peddling a bike, or a rocket booster.

Concept: Electricity is the flow of electrons in a closed circuit.

Activity: Electric Ball

The children form a circle and join hands (representing a closed circuit). The children are to move a soccer ball or similar type ball if a soccer ball is not available around the circle. The ball represents the current or flow of electrons. The children move the ball from one child to the next by using the instep of the foot as in soccer. The object of the game is to keep the ball moving around the circle and preventing the ball from leaving the circle by blocking it with the feet or legs while keeping the hands joined at all times. If the ball leaves the circle (an open or broken circuit), the two children between whom the ball escapes the circle are each given a point. The game continues with the children having the lowest scores as winners.

Application: Children are able to see this concept demonstrated in this game, that the flow of electrons through a closed circuit by passing the ball around the circle and that a broken circuit prevents the flow of electricity when the ball leaves the circle.

Concept: Electricity is the flow of electrons in a closed circuit

Activity: Current Relay

Children are arranged in teams in rows. Each child reaches back between his legs with his right hand and grasps the left hand of the child immediately in back of him. On a signal the teams thus joined together race to the goal line some 30 feet from the starting line and then race back to the starting line. The team finishing first with the line unbroken wins. A team should be made up of all boys or all girls.

Application: The joined hands of the members of the teams represent the closed circuit. As long as the circuit remains unbroken, electricity can flow (the children could move their feet and proceed with the race). If the circuit is broken, it has to be repaired (the children rejoin hands) before electricity can continue to flow and the team can move forward again.

Concept: Lightning is electricity

Activity: Lightning Relay

The class is divided into several teams. The first child on each team toes a starting line. On a signal he jumps. Someone marks the heel print of each jumper. The next child on each team steps forward to the heel mark of the first child, toes this mark, and jumps. This procedure is continued until every child on each team has jumped. The team having jumped the greatest distance wins.

Application: Each child is electricity of lightning jumping from one cloud to another. The concept of lightning being electricity gathering in a cloud and jumping to the ground or to another cloud can be noticed by the children as they dramatize it in the game.

Concept: Electricity flows along metal conductors and will not flow along nonmental conductors such as glass or rubber

Activity: Keep Away

If there is a large number of children they should form a circle. For a small group the children may spread out and form a square or five-sided figure. One child is chosen to be *It,* and he stands in the center. The other children throw a ball around the circle or across the square. They try to keep the ball away from *It* while he tries to get his hands on it. If *It* catches the ball, he changes places with the last child who threw it, and the game continues. If *It* is unable to get hold of the ball in a minute's time, another *It* can be chosen.

Application: The ball becomes the electricity, the ball throwers are the conductors, and *It* is a nonconductor who tries to interfere with the flow of electricity. Any time the nonconductor is successful in interfering, the current of electricity is interrupted. Children can be encouraged to find out the kind of materials that are nonconductors and several safety practices that have developed for those working around electricity, both in business and around the home.

Concept: A magnet attracts iron and steel

Activity: Link Tag

The children are scattered about the activity area. Two children are chosen to be the taggers. The taggers link hands and attempt to tag other children. All children tagged link hands between the first two taggers, the chain growing longer with each addition. Only the end children, the original taggers, may tag other children. Runners may crawl under the chain to escape being tagged, but any child who deliberately breaks the chain is automatically caught. The game continues until all the children are tagged. The last two children caught become the taggers for the next game.

Application: The taggers are the magnets, and the other children represent things made of iron or steel. As the taggers touch the other children by tagging, the children are attracted to them and become a part of the magnetic chain. It should also be pointed out that only the taggers at the ends of the chain can tag others, which demonstrates that magnets are strongest at the ends or poles.

Concept: The force of a magnet will pass through many materials

Activity: Hook-on Tag

One child is selected as a runner or magnet. The remaining children form groups of four. The children of each group stand one behind the other, each with arms around the waist of the child in front. Each group should be all boys or all girls. The runner attempts to hook on at the end of any column where he can. The group members twist and swing about, trying to protect the end person from being caught. If the runner is successful, the leader of that group becomes the new runner. The group having the most of its original members in it at the end of a specified period of time is the winner.

Application: Before starting the game, it should be pointed out that the runner in the game is the magnet. When he is successful in hooking on to the end of one of the groups, the power of the magnet travels through the group to the first person, who becomes the new magnet. This activity dramatizes that a magnet does not have to be in direct contact with another magnetic material in order to attract it. Later, children can be encouraged to experiment to determine which materials the force of a magnet will travel through.

Concept: Unlike poles of a magnet attract each other

Activity: North and South

The class is divided into two equal groups. The two groups line up facing each other about 10 feet apart midway between designated goal lines. One group is named North and the other one South. The teacher has a ten-inch square of cardboard which has N on one side and S on the other. The teacher throws the cardboard into the air between the teams where all can see where it lands. If the S side shows, the South team turns and runs to their goal line, chased by the North team. All who are tagged before reaching the line join North, and the two groups line up facing each other again. The cardboard is thrown into the air again, and the game continues in the same manner. The team which eliminates the other wins the game.

Application: The two groups represent the opposite or unlike poles of a magnet, the N and S poles. When one group turns to run to its goal line, it attracts the other group which pursues it.

Concept: When a magnet attracts an object, that object becomes a magnet

Activity: Magnet, Magnet

The children are divided into groups called pins, needles, paper clips, or anything else that can be attracted by a magnet. The groups stand behind a line at one end of the activity area. One child is selected to be the magnet and stands in the center of the activity area. The magnet calls, "Magnet, magnet I dare pins to come over" (or any of the other groups), whereupon all the children of that group run to the opposite side of the activity area. Magnet tries to catch them. Any child tagged must then help magnet whenever he calls another group to come over. The magnet may dare everybody over at one time or two groups at a time. The last child caught becomes the new magnet.

Application: The children should notice that the magnet, as he tags other children, causes them to become magnetized and have the power to magnetize others by tagging them. The magnet attracts others by calling to them.

SCIENCE PHYSICAL EDUCATION LISTENING AND READING CONTENT

Early attempts to develop science physical education stories were patterned after the original procedure used in providing for reading content discussed in Chapter 4. That is, several stories were written around certain kinds of physical education activities, the only difference being that the content also involved reference to science experiences. These stories were tried out in a number of situations. As in the case of the mathematics physical education stories, it soon became apparent that with some children the development of science concepts in a story was too difficult. The reason for this appeared to be that certain children could not handle both the task of reading while at the same time developing an understanding of the science aspect of the story. It was then decided that since listening is a first step in learning to read, auditory input should be utilized. This process involved having children listen to a story, perform the activity, and simultaneously try to develop the science concept that was inherent in the story. When it appeared desirable, this process was extended by having the children read the story after having engaged in the activity. Of course, with some children it was possible to have them begin just with the reading process.

Some examples of science physical education stories follow.

The first example concerns the game Shadow Tag which is played in the following manner: The players are dispersed over the playing area with one person designated as *It*. If *It* can step on or get into the shadow of another player, that player becomes *It*. A player can keep from being tagged by getting into the shade or by moving in such as way that *It* finds it difficult to step on his shadow. The story about this game is The Shadow Game.

The Shadow Game

Have you ever watched shadows?

When do you see your shadow?

What can your shadow do?

Here is a game to play with shadows.

You can play it with one or more children.

You can be *It*.

Tell your friends to run around, so you cannot step
    on their shadow.

When you step on a shadow, that child becomes *It*.

You join the other players

Could you step on someone's shadow?

In one specific situation at first grade level the story was used to introduce the concept that shadows are formed by sun shining on various objects. Following this a definition of a shadow was given. A discussion led the class to see how shadows are made as well as why they move. The class then went outside the room to where many kinds of shadows were observed. Since each child had a shadow it was decided to put them to use in playing the game.

In evaluating the experience, the teacher felt that the children saw how the sun causes shadows. By playing the game at different times during the day they also observed that the length of the shadow varied with the time of day. It was generalized that the story and the participation in the activity proved very good for illustrating shadows.

The next example involves the game Catch the Cane which is played as follows. The children stand in a line one beside the other. Each child is given a number. One child is *It* and stands in front facing the line of children. He places a stick or bat on the surface area in an upright position and balances it by putting his finger on top of it. *It* calls out one of the numbers assigned to the children in the line. At the same time he lets go of the stick. The child whose number is called dashes to get the stick before it falls to the surface area. *It* dashes to the place occupied by the child whose number was called. If the child gets the stick in time, he returns to his place in the line, and *It* holds the stick again. After the children have learned the game, several lines can be formed to provide active participation for more children. The following original story was written about this game.

Wilbur Woodchuck and His Cane

Wilbur Woodchuck hurt his leg.
He needed a cane.
At last his leg got better.
He did not need his cane.
He said, "I will find some friends.
We will play a game with my cane."
Wilbur's friends stood in line.
Wilbur was in front of the line.
He stood the cane in front of him.
He held it with his hand.
He called a friend's name.
Wilbur let the cane fall.
His friend caught it before it hit the ground.
He took Wilbur's place.
They played for a long time.
Could you find something to use for a cane and play
    this game with other children?

The story can be used to introduce a broad understanding of the force of gravity, with an application as follows. It can be pointed out that the stick in this game represents the object which is being acted upon by the force of gravity. Every time *It* lets go of the stick, the stick begins to fall to the ground. This demonstrates the concept of the force of gravity to children. They may be helped to notice that they must move faster than the force of gravity in order to catch the stick before it falls to the ground.

As mentioned previously, physical education stories can be written about stunts and rhythmic activities as well as games. As far as stunts are concerned, a good opportunity is offered for understanding in the broad area of *variety of life.* An example is shown in the story that follows involving the Camel Walk, which is concerned with understanding that animals move around in different ways.

Casper Camel

Casper Camel lives in the zoo.
He has a hump on his back.
Could you look like Casper Camel?
You will need a hump.
Try it this way.
Bend forward.
Put your hands behind your back.
Hold them together.
That will be a hump.
That will look like Casper Camel.
Could you move like Casper Camel?
Take a step.
Lift your head.
Take a step.
Lift your head.
Move like Casper Camel.
Do you think it would be fun to walk like Casper Camel?

One of the most desirable media for child expression through movement is found in rhythmic activities. One need only look at the functions of the human body to see the importance of rhythm in the life of the elementary school child. The heart beats in rhythm; the digestive processes function in rhythm; breathing is done in rhythm. In fact, almost anything in which human beings are involved is done in a more or less rhythmic pattern. As mentioned in Chapter 2 a very important aspect of rhythmic activities is the classification known as creative rhythms which are particularly important to our purpose here. Two stories are presented; the first story is oriented to the broad area of seasonal change.

Falling Leaves

Leaves fall.
They fall from the trees.
They fall to the ground.
Fall like leaves.
Down, down, Down.
Down to the ground.
Quiet leaves.
Rest like leaves.
Could you dance like falling leaves?

The second story is oriented to growth generally and to plant growth specifically.

The Growing Flowers

Flowers grow.
First they are seeds.
Be a seed.
Grow like a flower.
Grow and grow.
Keep growing.
Grow tall.
Now you are a flower.
Could you grow like a flower?

It is reiterated that it is highly recommended that teachers draw upon their own ingenuity and creativeness to prepare science physical education stories, instructions for which were given in Chapter 4.

Chapter 8

INTEGRATION OF
PHYSICAL EDUCATION AND SOCIAL STUDIES

Because of its possibilities of social development of children, physical education has often been referred to as the ideal laboratory for human relations. It has been demonstrated many times over that on the playfields racial and religious prejudices give way to cooperation and common endeavor for the benefit of the group. Indeed, children are perhaps more likely to judge their peers on their ability to perform physical education skills proficiently than they are to consider family background, color of skin, and the like as a basis for appraisal.

Some of the objectives of the social studies program in the elementary school include, among others, (1) to help children live by democratic processes, (2) to help children learn the procedures involved in problem solving, (3) to help children develop an appreciation of leadership and followership, and (4) to help children gain an understanding and appreciation of the customs and contributions of our own people as well as the people of other lands. Potential opportunities for acquiring these knowledges and appreciations are abundant in practically all phases of the elementary school physical education program. The following illustrative list suggests a number of general ways in which it is possible to integrate social studies and physical education experiences.

1. There are numerous physical education situations through which children may gain a better understanding of the importance of cooperation. By their very nature many games depend upon the cooperation of group members in achieving a common goal. Dancing is an activity that requires that persons perform together in a synchronization of rhythmical patterns. In skills such as throwing and catching there must be a coordinated action on the part of the thrower and the catcher. In certain kinds of stunts children work and learn together in groups of three, two children assisting the performer and then others taking turns performing. In these and

183

countless other situations the importance of working together for the benefit of the individual and the group is readily discerned.

2. It has been demonstrated on numerous occasions that children may gain an insight into the way of life of our own people and people of other lands by learning dances, stunts, and games engaged in by these people. In that play is perhaps the one best medium for child understanding, this procedure is a particularly noteworthy one. Early American country dances and nationality dances, as well as various kinds of period games and games from foreign lands, provide children with an opportunity to see the significance between the activities and the cultural and physical aspects that bear upon them.

3. Leadership and followership activities may be engaged in in such games as Follow the Leader. (One person is selected to be the leader and others follow him and attempt to do the same things that he does.)

4. Developing group consciousness and friendliness within a group can be accomplished in certain physical education activities. The natural opportunities for wholesome group experiences in games provide an opportunity for the development of ability to get along with various kinds of people. One teacher confronted with the problem of getting her fourth grade class to be more congenial employed the game Hook On (described previously but repeated here for purposes of continuity). In this game one player is selected to be *It* and and another is selected to be the Chaser. These two take positions at opposite ends of the activity area. The other players form couples by linking arms with a partner. The couples take places anywhere in the activity area. At a signal the Chaser attempts to tag *It*, who dodges in and out between the couples. In order to avoid being tagged, he can "hook on" to a free arm of one of the couples. In this event the other person of that couple becomes *It* and the game proceeds in this manner. The teacher found that this particular activity helped to eliminate certain cliques that were being formed in her class. She noticed too that children did not always hook on to their friends, since out of necessity they needed to hook on to any available couple to avoid being tagged.

5. Certain activities help to provide for an understanding of the meaning and need for boundaries and zones. Games that require a certain-sized playing space and that require that players stay in a

certain zone are helpful in interpreting the purpose of boundaries of countries, zoning in communities, and the like. It is more meaningful when children are given an opportunity to diagram and lay out play areas for certain kinds of activities.

6. Physical education activities provide an opportunity for planning and working together. Children are able to learn techniques of planning and working together when the teacher works with them in organizing and carrying out plans for their physical education activities.

7. Issues that might arise as a result of certain misunderstandings in physical education activities give rise to the exercise of wholesome social controls. The relationships of these social controls in physical education experiences to those in community living might possibly be understood in varying degrees by children at the different age levels. In these situations outstanding settings are provided for the development of problem-solving techniques in which children are placed in a position to make value judgments.

USE OF PHYSICAL EDUCATION IN SOCIAL STUDIES UNITS

When the history of education is considered over a period of several hundred years, the *unit* may be thought of as a more or less recent innovation. Because of this it is difficult to devise a universal definition for the term *unit.* This is partly due to the fact that the term does have a fixed meaning in the field of education. Essentially, the purpose of unitary teaching is to provide for a union of component-related parts which evolve into a systematic totality. In other words, the unit should consist of a number of interrelated learnings which are concerned with a specific topic or central theme. A variety of types of experiences as well as various curriculum areas are drawn upon for the purpose of enriching the learning medium for all children so that the understandings of the topic in question may be developed.

It will not be the purpose here to consider the advantages or disadvantages of the various types of units that have been discussed in textbooks and the periodical literature. On the contrary, it will be the purpose of this section of the chapter to discuss the role of physical education as a curriculum area to be "drawn upon for the purpose of enriching the learning medium for all children so that the understandings of the topic in question may be developed."

There is universal agreement among educators that the things that children do—the activities—are by far the most important part of the unit. Yet, those experiences through which children may learn best; that is, through active play experiences, have been grossly neglected as essential and important activities of the unit. However, there is an explanation for this paradoxical phenomenon. For example, the classroom teacher who should be well prepared to guide and direct many learning experiences and activities of the unit, may not feel confident enough to include physical education activities as a means of developing the concepts of the unit. Moreover, when there is a physical education specialist available to assist the classroom teacher, this individual may not be familiar enough with the other curriculum areas to recommend physical education activities to the classroom teacher that will be of value in developing the concepts of the unit. This does not mean to imply that this condition exists in all elementary schools because some elementary school physical educators are doing an outstanding piece of work in helping classroom teachers in the integration of physical education and social studies. Practices of this kind are to be commended; however, they take place in far too few cases. An examination of a large number of social studies units has indicated this to be true and perhaps due to the reasons mentioned above.

The reader should not interpret the previous discussion in the light that the recommendation of the use of physical education activities as learning activities of social studies is something new. In fact, on occasion this procedure has been recommended by persons outside the field of physical education. Over half century ago, Mossman[1] developed a list of the things that people do. These activities were classified into ten groups, with a total of some 80 different activities. It is interesting to note that some of the activities were concerned exactly with the "things children do" in physical education, such as *playing, dancing,* and *recreating.*

In order to show more clearly how physical education can be used as a means of extending the basis for learning in social studies units, a concrete example is submitted at this point.

This concerns how physical education activities can contribute to learning in social studies units involving the broad areas of *periods of*

[1]Mossman, Lois C., *The Activity Concept,* New York, The Macmillan Company, 1938, p. 54.

exploration, colonization, and *Western expansion* in the development of our country. This material was developed for social studies units taught in the fifth and sixth grades. Following is a sampling of the concepts of the units and the physical education activities used in the development of them.

Concept: Many people decided to settle in the western part of the country when lands were opened for homesteading; there were often exciting races for the choice sites.

Activity: Circle Run

In this activity the players form a circle and stand about six feet apart. All face counterclockwise. On a signal all start to run, keeping the general outline of the circle. As they run, each player tries to pass the runner in front of him on the outside. A player passing another tags the one passed and the one passed is out of the race. The last person left in the circle wins. On a designated signal from the teacher the circle turns and runs in a clockwise direction. This may occur at the decision of the teacher.

Concept: Many pioneers became famous for their deeds of courage and heroism

Activity: Famous Pioneers

One player selected to be *It* has a paper pinned on the back of his clothing upon which is written the name of a famous pioneer. All of the other players stand on a line facing *It,* who has turned around so that the other players can see his pioneer name. *It* asks questions of the players until he can identify his pioneer name by their answers. When *It* guesses the name, all players run to a line at the opposite end of the activity area. *It* tries to tag as many as he can before they get across the line. Players take turns being *It* and different pioneer names are used.

Concept: The colonists and pioneers needed great endurance and stamina in order to survive in the wilderness that was their new home.

Activity: Back-to-Back Pull

In this activity two boys of nearly equal size stand back to back, holding a stick with both hands over their heads. Each tries to pull the stick forward and across his own chest. Success often requires a great deal of strength and endurance. (A part of an old mop handle or broom handle can be used for the stick for this combative activity.)

Concept: Many of the skills and knowledges of the Indians were adopted by the white settlers (Indian scout pacing)

Activity: Scout Pace Relay

The class is divided into a number of equal groups and each group forms a column. On a signal the first person in each column travels to a given point and returns by alternating running and walking. He first runs 10 paces and then walks 10 paces, alternating this procedure until he returns to the original starting point. Each succeeding person in each column carries out this same procedure. The column finishing first wins.

PHYSICAL EDUCATION ACTIVITIES AS ESSENTIAL ASPECTS OF SOCIAL STUDIES UNITS

The previous discussion purported to indicate how physical education might serve as one of many subject-matter areas to provide activities to help in developing the understandings of a social studies unit. This section of the chapter pertains to those situations in which physical education activities might well be considered essentially responsible for the success of certain units. To illustrate this point, some practical examples follow. The first example pertains to a physical education activity which was an outgrowth of a fifth-grade social studies unit called "Living in Colonial Maryland." During one phase of this particular study, the children were divided into groups to explore the subject "Living, Working, and Playing in Colonial Days."

One group had as its problem "Good Times in Early Maryland." It was the job of this group to locate, read, and study any information on this subject and to share it with the class in any way they felt to be effective.

After three days of research and discussion, the children had listed many colonial activities, such as square dancing, handicap races, and husking bees. They had discovered that many of the good times in colonial days were based upon work. They read that husking bees were a very popular example of this, and that while the adults were husking corn, the children played games with the ears of corn. The group member then made up games and relays that the colonial boys and girls might have played at a husking bee. One of these was the Corn Race.

They decided to share their information with the other class members by having a colonial party at which they taught the games enjoyed by colonial children to the class. The "Food Group" joined them and served colonial refreshments at their party—popcorn and milk. The activity that the class preferred and requested many times afterward was the Corn Race.

In the Corn Race (a relay) the class is divided into a number of equal groups and each group forms a column. In front of each column a circle about three feet in diameter is drawn on the surface area to represent a corn basket. Straight ahead, beyond each of the corn baskets, four smaller circles are drawn about 10 feet apart. In each of the four small circles an object representing an ear of corn is placed. These objects may be blocks, beanbags, or the like. At a signal the first person in each column runs to the small circles in front of, and in line with, his column and picks up the corn one ear at a time and puts all of the ears in the corn basket. The second person takes the ears of corn from the basket and replaces them in the small circles. The third person picks them up and puts them in the basket, and the game proceeds until all members have run and returned to their places.

Another example shows how folk dances were used as a basis for an understanding of people of other lands. This particular class had been using a basal reader which took the children "on a tour" through six countries. As an introduction to the book the children were given a preview of these countries through travel posters and pictures. Each country was located on the map in an effort to give the children a beginning concept of life in countries beyond the boundaries of their own nation.

As study progressed, and the countries were "visited," many ideas were elicited from the children for learning more about the background and culture of these countries. This was done during the enrichment period of each reading lesson. A map of the world was used to advantage here. As each country was visited, a small flag of that country was presented and placed on the map. A small figure of a child in native costume was also added to this map project

One of the most enjoyable of these enrichment activities, from the children's point of view, was the learning of folk dances peculiar to the culture of the country being studied. The repertory of dances grew to such an extent that, as a part of the culminating activity of the year's work, the children decided to have a folk-dance fete, at which time they engaged in all of the folk dances previously learned. As a further outcome, since many of these dances were those required at the annual county-wide folk-dance festival, it placed the learning of them in a much more meaningful situation.

The motivation and background for the dances learned in connection with this unit were provided during the reading period. Consequently, it was possible to devote a large part of the physical education period to learning and participating in the dances.

SIMULATED TEACHING–LEARNING SITUATIONS

The following examples are intended to show how social studies and physical education can be successfully integrated in given teaching-learning situations. The first procedure illustrates how an activity called Kick the Beanbag was used with third grade children in studying Indians in connection with Columbus Day and Thanksgiving.

TEACHER: Yesterday, we learned how Shining Star and his men enjoyed fishing and hunting. In what other ways did they enjoy themselves?

CHILD: They had feasts and played games and danced.

TEACHER: Yes, we found out they liked to have many feasts, and to play games and to dance. The Indians, both young and old, played games; even the women played, too. The children played all the games of the grown people.

CHILD: Did the Indian kids play any games like we do?

TEACHER: Well, yes, the Indians were particularly good at racing and would often run over a thirty-mile course.

CHILD: Wow! that's a long way to run.

TEACHER: Sometimes they ran in teams with each other, kicking a ball of wood or pine gum the size of a croquet ball with their bare feet. They also had relay races in which the runners went back and forth on a straight track. Each runner had to make one full trip. Another game was hoop and pole. Here the player rolled a hoop along the ground and each player threw a stick or a spear toward it.

CHILD: I'll bet that was fun.

TEACHER: They also had plenty of hiding games, such as hiding a pebble in a moccasin or a bean in a hill of sand. (*The teacher continues, holding a bean in hand.*) Do you know anything about this little bean?

CHILD: It grows in the ground.

TEACHER: Yes, and let me tell you something else about it. This little bean's forefather was first raised by some Indians of Peru. That was a long time ago because back in 1492, when Columbus first came to America, he did not know what they were, but he and his followers soon found they were good to eat. The Indian women taught them how to bake beans in underground holes, and how to make bean soup.

CHILD: We had bean soup in the cafeteria today.

TEACHER: Yes, we still eat some of the same kinds of food today. Now, after the Pilgrims settled at Plymouth, Massachusetts, they soon made friends with the Indians. What do you suppose the children began to do?

CHILD: Did they play games with them?

TEACHER: Yes, they gathered these beans and sewed them in bags of cloth or skins to make a ball to kick or throw. Today we do the same thing and call them beanbags. (*Teacher holds up a beanbag.*)

CHILD: Gee, not a bad idea.

TEACHER: After the Pilgrims had been here a year they had a feast. What was it called?

CHILD: Thanksgiving.

TEACHER: Do you suppose we could make believe we are Indians and Pilgrims at the first Thanksgiving feast playing one of our favorite games? Let's try it for part of our physical education period. (*Class goes to the all-purpose room for physical education and the teacher continues.*)

TEACHER: Let's divide the class into Indians and Pilgrims. Everyone count off by fours. Now the 1s, 2s, 3s, and 4s each please form a column. Fine, now columns 1 and 3 will be the Indians and columns 2 and 4 will be the Pilgrims. (*The children organize and the teacher continues.*) Remember, we said that the Indians played a game by kicking a ball of wood or pine gum with their bare feet. The game we are going to play is called Kick the Beanbag, but we are going to kick it with our shoes on. We will use the same lines that we have for other relays. When I say, "Go!" the first player from each team starts to kick the beanbag that has been placed in front of his column. He must kick it with his right foot only. He kicks it toward the line at the other end of the room. When he reaches the line, he must start back, using the left foot only. When he gets back to his team, the second player starts out, and so on. The team having all of its players back in place is the winner. Let's have the first column show us how. (*Some of the children in the first column demonstrate and the teacher further explains until all understand. The relay is run and the teacher evaluates it with them.*)

TEACHER: How was that relay like a game played by the Indians?

CHILD: It was a little like where they kicked the wooden ball with their bare feet.

CHILD: They also ran relays.

TEACHER: Yes, and what do you have to do to help your team win?

CHILD: Well, for one thing, you have to kick the beanbag straight.

TEACHER: Yes indeed, that certainly is important. How might we improve this relay if we were to do it again?

CHILD: Try to kick a little way instead of kicking it so hard.

CHILD: When some kids kicked it real hard it went the wrong way and they had to go away from their line to get it.

CHILD: Yes, and sometimes they got in the other kids' way.

CHILD: Could we kick it with first the right foot and then the left foot instead of with the right foot all the way up and the left foot all the way back?

TEACHER: I think we could try that another time. All of your suggestions are good and perhaps we can think of more ideas before we play it again.

The learning of folk dances and something about their use in a country help children understand people of other lands and different cultures. In the geography-of-the-world aspect of social studies at the upper elementary level, there is a good opportunity to develop an understanding that the basic needs of people are much the same the world over, and that their needs are satisfied according to the resources at hand. It can be shown how the desire for relaxation and fun is met in part through folk dancing by people of other lands. The following procedures illustrates how this was accomplished with a group of fourth grade children through the folk dance, *Cshebogar*. (There are a number of appropriate recordings that can be used for accompaniment for this dance.)

The group forms a single circle, with boys and girls alternating. Boys stand to the left of their girl partners. Hands are joined. The following movements are made with the indicated measures of the accompaniment.

1. Eight slides clockwise.	Measures 1–4
2. Eight slides counterclockwise	Measures 5–8
3. With the hands joined and held above the head four walking steps are taken toward the center of the circle. Hands are lowered and four steps are taken back to place.	Measures 9–10 Measures 11–12
4. Partners do a Hungarian Turn. This is done by facing each other and placing right hands around the other's waist while the left arms are extended	Measures 13–16

high with elbows straight. (Partners pull away or lean slightly from each other during this move-movement.) Skip eight times, turning counterclockwise.

5. Partners, facing each other with hands joined, slide sideways (closing with opposite foot) toward the center of the circle four times.　　　　　　　　Measures 17–20

   This movement is reversed by the partners sliding back to the outside of the circle.　　　　　Measures 21–24

6. Same as above except *two* slides to center and *two* slides back to position.　　　　　　　Measures 25–28

7. Partners do the Hungarian Turn.　　　　　Measures 29–32

TEACHER: How many of you remember singing the song "Quite Different"? (*Several children raise hands and teacher continues.*) I thought many of you would recall it. From what country did it come to us?

CHILD: Was it Czechoslovakia?

TEACHER: Czechoslovakia is right, Sam. Do any of you know of other music that tells us about Czechoslavakia?

CHILD: There is "Bright Morava."

TEACHER: Fine. Anything else.

CHILD: We had "The Moldau."

TEACHER: Good. I was sure you would mention those because you have said they were favorites. Today we are going to learn a folk dance of a country that is a next door neighbor of Czechoslovakia. The country is Hungary. I have written the name of the dance on the board. Who would like to pronounce it? (*One or two children try to pronounce it and the teacher continues.*) It is pronounced She-bō-gär. Let's all say it.

TEACHER AND CHILDREN: Cshebogar.

TEACHER: The village people and farmers of Hungary have always enjoyed dancing because there is little else to do for amusement. On wedding days, during the wine festivals, and on holidays they put on their best clothes and celebrate. Gypsy bands of musicians sometimes provide the music. In Hungary there is very little entertainment that does not include music. Now let's listen to the music for our dance, Cshebogar, and see if it tells us what to do. (*The record accompaniment is played and the dance is taught step by step, as indicated in the previous description. After the children have participated in the dance, the teacher evaluates it with them.*)

TEACHER: Did you notice any rough spots in our dancing today, Joyce?

CHILD: We were crowded when we walked to the center of the circle the first time.

TEACHER: What could we do about that?

CHILD: If we all took smaller steps, there would be plenty of room for everyone.

TEACHER: That's a very good suggestion. We all want to be comfortable when we dance. Susan, what did you notice?

CHILD: We-l-l, my partner didn't skip to the music on the Hungarian Turn. He went so fast I almost slipped and fell.

TEACHER: We want to avoid accidents, to be sure. What can we do to be safe on the turns? John? (*Susan's partner.*)

CHILD: I guess we should listen to the music, because it tells you how fast to go.

TEACHER: Yes, it certainly does. Anything else?

CHILD: Some of us didn't think ahead to the next step and we weren't ready to change.

TEACHER: What can we do about that?

CHILD: I guess we have to review all the steps in order before we dance again.

TEACHER: We can do that next time. Is there anything about this dance you especially like?

CHILD: The Hungarian Turn.

TEACHER: That is fun to do, and I am sure that the people who dance it in Hungary enjoy it just as you do. Joe, do you want to tell us something else you liked about it?

CHILD: I like to change directions often like we did in this dance.

CHILD: In the part where you walk into the circle and back, I felt like I wanted to stamp my foot on the last step. Also, maybe we could yell out "Hi!" after each Hungarian Turn.

TEACHER: Yes, that sounds like something we might try.

CHILD: I think this is a happy dance. You can have a good time doing it.

TEACHER: Yes, and the Hungarians danced the Cshebogar on happy occasions. Perhaps soon we can talk about some other ways this dance is done and try them.

PHYSICAL EDUCATION ACTIVITIES
WITH INHERENT SOCIAL STUDIES CONCEPTS

Social studies concepts are inherent in many physical education activities. Inasmuch as the social studies involve topics or themes that are often closely related to the immediate environment and interests of children, there is a natural setting for integration of this curriculum area and physical education. It has been demonstrated in numerous cases that a better understanding of concepts in certain social studies topics can be attained through participation in physical education activities. The selected physical education activities that appear in the following section of the chapter have been used successfully in practical situations for this purpose.

Concepts: People communicate by telephone, newspaper, radio, television, and so on; the radio brings us news. (Communication)

Activity: Air Raid

The children form a double circle, all facing the center. One child acts as the "radio voice." He is *It* and he takes his place in the center of the circle. When *It* calls out "Air raid," the inside circle walks, skips, or runs clockwise within the circle. When *It* calls, "All clear," the players immediately stop in front of another player in the outside circle. *It* attempts to find a partner and the player left without a partner selects the player to be the "radio voice" for the next time. Each time the game is played, the inside and outside circles are alternated.

Concept: Man travels by automobile (Transportation)

Activity: Automobile

The children sit in chairs arranged in a circle. Each child is given the name of a part of an automobile, such as the wheel, hub, axle, and the like. The teacher or a child begins the game by telling a story about the automobile, bringing in the parts of it. As each part is mentioned, the child or children involved get up and run around the chair. At some point in the story, the storyteller calls out "Automobile." At this point everyone must leave his seat and get a different one, with the storyteller trying also to get one of the seats. The person who does not get a seat can become the next storyteller or a point can be scored against him, as the children decide.

Concept: Many stores provide us with clothing; we can buy clothes at a department store (Clothing)

Activity: Department Store

All children are seated, with the exception of five or six who stand in a line in front of the class. Each of the players standing in the line selects the name of a person who works in a department store, such as clerk, manager, cashier, buyer, and the like. The players who are seated close their eyes and those in the line change from their original places. After this rearrangement the children in the seats are told to open their eyes and they attempt to give the names of the new arrangement. The first child to raise his hand is given an opportunity to try. If he misses a point is scored against him, and if he succeeds he scores a point. Leaders or "store workers" are changed each time.

Concept: Man travels by train (Transportation)

Activity: Railroad Train

One child is selected to be the trainmaster and another to be the starter. The rest of the children are given names of parts of a train, workers, kinds of trains, or objects carried on a train. The trainmaster then tells a story, using the names that have been given to the children. When a child's train name is mentioned, he runs to the starter and stands behind him, putting his hands on the shoulders or hips of the child in front of him. When all have become a part of the train, or whenever the starter wishes, he gives the starting whistle and the train starts moving around the activity area. The starter leads the train wherever he wishes to go.

Concept: Cats frighten mice (Pets)

Activity: Pussy Cat

This activity is done to the words of the nursery rhyme "Pussy Cat, Pussy Cat, Where Have You Been?" The words as well as the music can be found in various record accompaniment sources. The children form a circle, with one child selected as the Pussy Cat taking his place in the middle of the circle. The children in the circle sing lines 1 and 3 and the child in the center (Pussy Cat) sings lines 2 and 4.

1. Pussy cat, pussy cat, where have you been? (Children in the circle join hands and walk counterclockwise around the circle.)
2. I've been to London to visit the Queen. (Children in the circle change direction and walk clockwise around the circle.)
3. Pussy cat, pussy cat, what did you there? (Children in the circle drop hands and walk four steps to the center of the circle toward Pussy Cat.)
4. I frightened a little mouse under the chair. (On the last word of the verse, "chair," the children in the circle run to a previously desig-

nated safe place while Pussy Cat tries to tag as many as he can before they reach safety.)

Concept: Man can travel by water (Transportation)
Activity: Row, Row, Row Your Boat

The words and music to "Row, Row, Row Your Boat" are found in many of the standard music books used at the elementary school level. The children stand in four rows and place their hands on the shoulders of the child in front of them. The children in each row sing one or more rounds of the song. The following action is carried out as each row begins its first round of singing.

1. Row, row, row your boat. (The first row of children takes four steps forward in unison.)
2. Gently down the stream. (The second row of children takes four steps forward and the first row takes four steps backward to its original place.)
3. Merrily, merrily, merrily, merrily, (The third row of children takes four steps forward, and the second row takes four steps backward, and the first row takes four steps forward.)
4. Life is but a dream. (The fourth row of children takes four steps forward, the third row takes four steps backward, the second row takes four steps forward, and the first row takes takes four steps backward.)

This procedure is continued until all of the rounds have been sung. All rows will then be back in their original positions.

Concept: Understanding meaning of equator, Artic Circle, and Antartic Circle (Geography)
Activity: Equator

The class forms a large circle in the center of the activity area. A line is drawn around the circle in front of the players. This area is called the equator. The class then divides into three equal groups. One of the groups remains in the equator circle. The second group goes to one end of the activity area and draws a circle with a marker. The third group follows the same procedure at the other end of the activity area. The circle at the "north" end of the area is known as the North Pole and the circle at the "south" end as the South Pole. A ball is given to each of the groups at the North Pole and the South Pole. They try to hit the players in the equator below the waist with the ball. Players hit with the ball must go into the area from which they were hit. Teams rotate so that each team has an opportunity to be in the equator region. At the end of a specified time the team having the most players in the center (equator) wins the game.

Concept: Understanding that there are seven continents (Geography)

Activity: Explorer

The children are seated in a circle with one player in the center of the circle. Each player selects the name of one of the continents and tells its name. (Several children will have the name of the same continent.) The "Explorer," standing in the center of the circle, calls out the name of two continents. The children who have these names must get up and get a different seat. The explorer tries to get a seat and the player left without a seat selects the explorer for the next time.

Concept: The pioneers were sturdy people and sometimes they had to fight unfriendly Indians (Colonial Life)

Activity: Scouts and Indians

The class is divided into two teams. Two lines are drawn parallel about 25 to 30 feet apart, with each team standing behind each of the lines. The area between the two lines is the neutral area. One team is called the Scouts and the other team is called the Indians. The Scouts' territory is called the Stockade and the Indians' territory is called the Indian Village. Either Scouts or Indians venture into the neutral area, and when they do they run the risk of being caught by the "enemy." Members of either team, either individually or in small groups, attempt to bring opponents back to their own territory. That is, the Indians try to capture the Scouts and take them to the Indian Village and the Scouts try to capture the Indians and take them to the Stockade. The team with the greatest number of prisoners after a specified playing time is the winner. (If players fail to venture into the neutral area, the teacher should devise a signal denoting that a certain number of them should go into that area; otherwise, the objective of the game is lost.)

In summary, the book contains over 160 physical education activities suitable for use with the integration of reading, other language arts, mathematics, science or social studies. All of the activities have been extensively field tested and can be used successfully for integration when applied in the appropriate manner.

BIBLIOGRAPHY

Bradfield, R. H., et al, Run to learn—learn to run: Exercise as a behavior and academic facilitator, *The Physical Educator*, Winter 1989.

Brophy, K. and Hancock, S., The role of the teacher in facilitating social integration, *Early Child Development and Care*, 39, 1988.

Buschner, C. A., Role conflict for elementary classroom teachers: Teaching physical education, *The Physical Educator*, Summer 1985.

Croce, R. and Lavay, B., Now more than ever: Physical education for the elementary school-aged child, *The Physical Educator*, Spring 1985.

Elliot, M. E., Concept learning in elementary physical education, *Strategies*, January 1990.

Gabbard, C., Health related fitness: Curriculum formats for elementary physical education, *Strategies*, January 1990.

Espiritu, J. K., Quality physical education programs—cognitive emphasis, *Journal of Physical Education, Recreation and Dance*, August 1987.

Gentry, V. S., Curricular models of elementary physical education: Traditional and contemporary, *The Physical Educator*, Spring 1985.

Grant, B. C., Student behavior in physical education lessons: A comparison among student achievement groups, *The Journal of Educational Research*, March/April 1989.

Grice, G. L., and Jones, M. A., Teaching thinking skills: State mandates and the K–12 curriculum *Clearing House*, April 1989.

Humphrey, J. H., *Child Development and Learning Through Dance*, New York, AMS Press, Inc., 1987.

Humphrey, J. H., *Teaching Gifted Children Through Motor Learning*, Springfield, Illinois, Charles C Thomas Publisher, 1985.

Humphrey, J. H., Use of motor activity learning in the development of advanced academic skills and concepts with gifted and talented primary level children, Maryland Conference on Gifted and Talented Education, Baltimore 1984.

Humphrey, J. H. and Humphrey, J. N., *Reading Can Be Child's Play*, Springfield, Illinois, Charles C Thomas Publisher, 1990.

Humphrey, J. H. and Humphrey, J. N., *Mathematics Can Be Child's Play*, Springfield, Illinois, Charles C Thomas Publisher, 1990.

Humphrey, J. H. and Humphrey, J. N., *Help Your Child Learn the 3Rs Through Active Play*, Springfield, Illinois, Charles C Thomas Publisher, 1980.

Humphrey, J. N., and Humphrey, J. H., *Child Development During the Elementary School Years*, Springfield, Illinois, Charles C Thomas Publisher, 1989.

Is it better to have double classes taught by the physical education specialist than single classes taught by the classroom teacher? (discussion), *Journal of Physical Education Recreation and Dance,* March 1989.

Jacobs, L. B., The integration approach, Early Years, January 1987.

Jewette, A. E., Curriculum theory in physical education, *International Review of Education,* 35, 1989.

Kelly, L. E., Instructional time: The overlooked factor in PE curriculum development, *Journal of Physical Education, Recreation and Dance,* August 1989.

McEvers, J. and Blazer, S., Specialists enhance physical education curriculum, *Thrust,* September 1988.

Margrotta, J. R., Using conceptual themes for skill and fitness development, *Journal of Physical Education, Recreation and Dance,* November/December 1988.

Melle, M. and Wilson, F., Balanced instruction through an integrated curriculum, *Educational Leadership,* April 1984.

Ross, J. G., et al, What is going on in the elementary physical education program? *Journal of Physical Education, Recreation and Dance,* November/December, 1987.

Webster, G. E., Coordinating curriculum in physical education, *The Education Digest,* March 1989.

Weiss, M. R., and Klint, K. A., "Show and tell" in the gymnasium: An investigation of developmental differences in modeling and verbal rehearsal of motor skills, *Research Quarterly for Exercise and Sport,* September 1987.

INDEX